Grassland Plant ID for Everyone

for Everyone

*Except Folks That Take
Boring Technical Stuff Too Seriously*

By Jim Koweek
Photos by Dale Armstrong

RAFTER
LAZY K
PUBLISHING

ISBN: 978-1-4951-9470-2

Printed in the USA

Photography:
Dale Armstrong
dgastrong@gmail.com

Design:
Jon Kandel
JonKandel@me.com

Dedicated to Annette & Allyson —
Somehow they put up with us.

Also to my Dad, Arthur Koweek,
who probably doesn't know
how much he has inspired me
and how much I have learned from him.

Table of Contents

Grassland Plant ID For Everyone

Some folks look at verdant rolling grasslands, wrap themselves in the beauty and for them, that is enough. Others, probably most of us, want to know what the heck they are looking at and how it all works together. Unfortunately, we lack the time, discipline, and resources to dedicate years of our lives to obtaining that knowledge. Well, here is some good news for you — *Grassland Plant ID* is the ultimate shortcut to that deep knowledge. This book is like a weight loss pill for botanical knowledge that really works.

A Short Introduction

Grasses are part of the plant community in almost every life zone here in the great Southwest. You will see them at all elevations and locations, from the low deserts (after it rains) to the coldest, snowiest Alpine regions. In most places, they make up an important understory — kind of a carpet — under the dominant vegetation. But here in the grasslands, grasses rule. When I started on this project, it was going to be a grass identification field guide. Then it hit me like a lightning bolt in a summer thunderstorm. The grasslands aren't just about grasses. Trees, shrubs, and forbs all play roles here. That is why they are included.

I have sat around many a fascinating discussion of people talking about what exactly to call a plant community dominated by grasses. Well, "fascinating" might be slightly overstating it. Let's just say they were interesting at the time. Do we live in the grassland, desert grassland, or semi-arid grassland? In other parts of the world, (yes, grasslands occur in many parts of the world) this basic vegetation community might be called steppes, savannahs, or pampas. Personally, I am happy with just grasslands, or in poor moisture years I might use semi-arid grassland. Any use of the word "desert" implies 10" of rain or less, and that amount isn't going to support large stands of perennial grasses. In America we talk about two types of grasslands. The Midwestern prairie gets more moisture than the Southwestern grasslands. Of course the extra moisture allows bigger species to grow, so you could think of it as tall grass grasslands versus short grass grasslands.

The conditions that create a grassland in the Southwest and allow it to flourish are pretty unique. This set of conditions mainly occurs in elevations between about 3500' – 6000'. They exist between higher levels of desert scrub and lower areas of oak woodland. Grasslands need good summer moisture and expect cold, with some freezing nights, in the winter. Plants here have to be able to take extremes in weather and climate to survive. They can go months with no moisture or, if you are lucky, it might rain every day for two weeks in the summer rainy system. Much of the typical lower desert flora can't handle the cold, and higher elevation vegetation won't take the drought. For grasses, it is the "Goldilocks Zone," just right.

Of course, what is currently grasslands hasn't always been grasslands. During the last Ice Age, grasslands could be found lower in elevation and what now is grassland was wooded. If moisture patterns were to change and it got hotter and dryer, you could expect the desert scrub vegetation to move higher in elevation. This would result in plants with more thorns and spines in what now is grasslands. If the next Ice Age were to somehow start, the opposite would happen — grasslands would become wooded and desert scrub would get grassier. Don't hold your breath waiting for that one to happen.

It is hard to tie grasslands down to an exact elevation. You might think that's because location, exposure, and soil types all have major effects on what grows in an area. You would be right. But also it is because plants are living things and tend to break almost every rule out there. You don't want to read that "this plant occurs from 3500' – 6000'" and rule out an identification because the GPS says you are at 3300'. What might be good to remember is that all of Dale's excellent pictures were taken in southeastern Arizona between about 3200' – 6025'.

Young Mearns Quail

A Not-So-Short Introduction

Back in the fall of 2008, I had the chance to train up to perform the underappreciated but necessary task of Rangeland Monitoring. Rangeland Monitoring is a combination of methods that look at an area, often grazed by cattle, and give a non-biased scientific assessment of the trends in vegetation. It is a good tool for ranchers and agencies like the Forest Service or Bureau of Land Management to help manage land and keep it healthy. For me, it was a great opportunity (and a job). Most monitoring is done in the fall when my other work slowed down and it was a good chance to see some beautiful country that few others get to see.

The basic technique for the monitoring that we were doing involved going to an established point, taking some photos and placing a 14" square frame on the ground and identifying everything in it. Then move the frame one pace and repeat the identification process. We did that one hundred times per site. For some agencies, it was two hundred times. Two things became apparent in a hurry. First, I didn't know as much as I thought I did about plant identification. It is easy to walk in to an area and pick out the stuff you know and ignore the rest of it. This job called for knowing everything, not just acting like I knew everything. The second thing I learned is that it is good to have a high tolerance for redundant tasks.

No problem. I thought I would just read up on plants, and then I would know everything. Local researcher Jane Bock stopped by the nursery I owned at the time and tried to help out by giving me a book called Manual of the Grasses of the United States by A.S. Hitchcock. It is a very thorough book, and I believed my problems were over. They were... until I opened the book. For the common species Blue Grama, part of the description read, "Fertile lemma pilose, the intermediate lobes acute; rudiment densely bearded at the summit of the rachilla." I tried "Press 1 for English," no help. It was pretty dang obvious that I didn't know my "densely bearded rudiment" from my "pilose." There had to be another way to learn it all.

Fortunately, there was some great — and very patient — help available locally (more on that in the Acknowledgements section) and after a few monitoring seasons, grassland plant ID got a little easier. Seeing the same plants year after year gave them a sense of familiarity and soon, based on image clues rather than a technical dichotomous key, the plant vocabulary took off. At some point, I realized that plant identification was a lot like playing music. Some folks can read music and others play by ear. I was definitely a play it by ear kind of guy. To this day, I can now identify a number of plants but still have no clue what the Sam Hill a "densely bearded rudiment" is.

How To Use This Book

The plants in this book are all found in the grasslands of Arizona and New Mexico. We have tried to include not just the common species, but also unique ones that could have a role in native plant landscaping. Some of the plants are not spectacular by themselves, but when massed give the grasslands its rich, green feel in the summer rainy season. These overlooked plants need love too. Moisture, exposure, soil type, and location are going to determine what plants grow in an area. Except for a couple of trees, we have not included riparian plants. The vegetation in and around perpetually wet zones is totally different from the rest of the grasslands. It could be its own "Riparian Plant ID" book.

Let's not kid ourselves. The best way to identify a plant is to ask someone who knows their stuff to tell us what it is and explain a little about it. However, this technique comes with a warning. Many plant people have a speech issue. They can't say the words, "I don't know." Usually, they (we) say, "It could be," or "Reminds me of..." when the truth is we have no clue what it is. I have found the more someone really knows, the more likely they are to say, "I don't know." This is just something to be aware of.

Our goal with this book is that you can find a plant you are interested in, open it up and figure out what it is. This is a picture book. Upon occasion you might need more than the proverbial "1,000 words" to figure out a specimen. Because of that, we have included some basic information about each plant. You will find the maximum height, life cycle, whether the plant is native or introduced, the date the photo was taken, and a few other clues that will help with identification. Other plants in the picture are also identified. Heights are all in feet and inches. This is the Great Southwest of America. None of that metric stuff here.

One more final thought about the plant descriptions — and it may be the most important fact in the book. Plants can't read. They are bad about following rules. There will be exceptions to almost every "fact" here. Green Sprangletop is a large grass that averages 3' – 4' when flowering. However, I have seen it flower out at both 6' and at 6". That doesn't matter, it still is Green Sprangletop.

Names: Or to paraphrase Old Willie Shakespeare, By Any Other Name would a Bastardsage smell as sweet?

We have chosen to use common names for the plants. Rabbitbrush is referred to as Rabbitbrush and not *Ericameria nauseosus,* which is its botanical name. As my old pal the late Dave Eppele used to say, "Botanical names should only be used to clear things up, not confuse people." Most of the time, a mesquite tree should be called a mesquite tree and not *Prosopis velutina.* However, there are a couple of mesquites that grow in the grasslands, and the botanical names can help you be specific as to which one you are talking about. Sometimes there are identification clues in botanical names. The Mexican Blue Oak is *Quercus oblongifolia. Oblongifolia* means oblong leaf, which is what the Mexican Blue Oak has and is a characteristic that can help you tell it apart from the Arizona White Oak. The native Long Flowered Four O'Clock is *Mirabilis longiflora.* Of course longiflora means long flower. There is only one botanical name for each plant. With all the new work being done on DNA, many plants are being reclassified and renamed at a rate unheard of in the past (see Acacias). I can almost guarantee that between the time ink goes down on this page and the time it dries, some names will have changed. Sorry about that.

Sometimes a person can have more than one name. Robert, Bobby, and Boogerhead might all refer to the same individual. Plants are the same way and often names get localized. I have heard the names Native Sumac, Three Leaf Sumac, Wild Gooseberry, Squawbush, Lemonade Berry, and Skunkbush all referring to the same plant, *Rhus trilobata.* The US Department of Agriculture's Plant Database is the authority on botanical names. It lists the official botanical and official common name for each plant. Although many of the USDA Plant Database's common

names are seldom, if ever, used, I have included them to make looking up a particular plant easier. For some reason the USDA seems to have an obsession with "worts." For our purposes, we will go with the most accepted common name but will include others if they are helpful (or amusing). I promise to let you know if I make up any names.

Grasses – Not Just for Cattle Anymore

Originally, this book was going to be just about grass species identification. Many early grassland ID books focused solely on grasses and their relationship to the livestock industry. The 1952 University of Arizona publication *Common Arizona Range Grasses* is typical. It lists a species, gives a short physical description, then describes where it occurs. That is followed by a paragraph on forage value and management. No other benefits of the grasses are listed. Livestock interaction is a tremendously important component of grassland function. This is especially true if you like to see wide open spaces kept open and relatively undeveloped. Also true if you like a good burger. These days, for most folks, it is pretty obvious that the grasslands are way more than grasses and their protein content. Erosion control, water quality, wildlife habit and food, and even aesthetics all have a strong relationship with grassland plants. You don't have to have a 200 section ranch to benefit or appreciate grassland plants. Most of us have some plantings around the house. There are many grassland species that do well in domestication and thrive in a home landscape situation. This goes for many of the species listed here, not just grasses. These plants tend to require much less maintenance (work) than exotic species. I mention some of the species that have landscape potential but don't take my word for it. There is a lot out there. Think about what might be fun to have around and give it a try.

Using native plants around your property often gets you twice the bang for the buck. Many species attract hummingbirds, butterflies, or other interesting lifeforms. Desert Honeysuckle blooms when hummingbirds are migrating. Same thing for many of the penstemon species. Attracting hummingbirds is a good thing. In addition to pollinating plants, they eat gobs of insects every day, including mosquitos and gnats. Besides, who doesn't like seeing hummingbirds? I can't remember the last time I heard someone say, "Ma, get the rifle. That dang hummingbird is back!" Rabbitbrush is about the only thing flowering in the late fall. I have counted more than ten different species of butterflies on it at one time. I have often seen wild turkeys and quail feeding and hiding in patches of native grasses. When is the last time you have seen an oriole feeding on a hybrid Tea Rose? Reviewing the list of included plants made me aware of how many of our native plants attracted butterflies. To be truthful, butterflies have never been at the top of my interest list. However, if for the same amount of work, effort, and expense I can plant something I like looking at and it attracts butterflies, I am all in. The side benefit is that these types of plantings help the overall butterfly populations, some of which are really hurting. It would be nice if all problems were this easy to solve.

Hummingbird sp. on Tree Tobacco

Making More of 'Em

Wanting to work with native plants and finding them available commercially are two different things. Nurseries are a commercial venture. The ones that sell native plants always walk the line between what the owners like and what they think will sell. At least, the ones that stay in business walk that line. The good news is that selections are a lot better now than they were 20 or 30 years ago. If the demand is there, the supply will eventually catch up. It is a lot like "organic" food was 20 years ago, when the only place to buy anything organic was some little hippie store that smelled of patchouli oil, usually located on a back street. Now every chain grocery store has a large "organic" section.

Big box hardware stores basically stink as places to find unique native plants. I asked a manager of a large box type hardware store nursery why he didn't stock more native plants. Obviously, they would perform better than the exotics he had in stock. He told me he would like to, but was given a catalog of nurseries, mostly from out of state, and could only order from those sources. That is why you have citrus and bougainvillea sold at locations in southeastern Arizona at the 5000' elevation. There isn't going to be supply without the demand, so you might as well start asking and rewarding the local growers that do carry native material with your business.

The good news is that some of these plants are out there if you know where to look. Start with botanical garden or museum sales. They usually have small amounts of hard to find plants. If there is a native plant group or garden club, contact them. Small hobbyist nurseries are always fun too. Most plant people are very willing to share or trade.

Some of these plants just aren't going to be available. If you have decided to plant something unavailable, you are probably going to have to propagate it yourself. Now what follows this is by no means meant to be a complete guide to plant propagation. People dedicate whole careers to this subject and much has been written on it. I only bring it up to show it can be done, and sometimes it is not hard. Here are a few examples. We can use Wooly Bunch Grass and Cochise Beardtongue, as I am guessing they aren't the Blue Light Special at the K-Mart Garden department this week.

Most grasses can be propagated two different ways. If you are going the seed route, remember there is an unbreakable formula for success. Good seed + warm ground temperature (approximately 80 degrees) + sufficient moisture = germination. Most native grass seed needs to stay constantly moist for over a week to germinate. This is the hard part of the equation.

In the wild, grass seed is dropped in late summer or fall. It blows around until it stops in a "safe site," usually under a rock or branch, in a depression, or under another plant. There, it is settled in by the gentle winter moisture (unless there isn't any gentle winter moisture, like there hasn't been for most of the last 20 years). There it waits in its "safe site" until the summer rains germinate it. Best guess is that native grass seed can lay dormant for 10 years or more, waiting for the right conditions. If you want to start Woolly Bunchgrass from seed you will probably have to collect it yourself. Once you have the seed, break up the ground to a depth of a few inches. Broadcast the seed and very lightly cover it. Most native grass seed doesn't like to be covered more than a quarter inch, so less is better. If native grass seed is covered too deep, it will not germinate. Keep it constantly moist for at least a week. Better yet, do this in late June and try to work with the summer rains. Then hope for the best.

The second method of propagating native grasses is a lot more reliable and quicker. Find a clump of Wooly Bunchgrass. Water it for a couple of days. Once the plant is well hydrated, (and the digging is easier) simply stick your shovel in and dig out part of that clump. Make sure you get some good roots with your section. Move it where you want it and water it in. Instant Wooly Bunchgrass. Just a note of caution to make sure you have permission to take whatever plant you are digging. The National Forests and State Lands kind of frown on folks taking their shovels out and digging, even if it is for personal consumption.

As for the Cochise Beardtongue, you are going to have to go the seed route on this one. This particular plant flowers in late summer. Like many plants that flower in the late summer rains or fall, this seed will need a period of colder temperatures in order to germinate. It makes sense in the natural world that a plant that produces seeds late in the growing season doesn't want them germinating right before the cool season. The seedlings would be very small and not make it through the winter. This process of having cold temperatures break dormancy is called cold stratification and is easy to duplicate using your fridge as a cold source. Just put the seeds in a zip lock bag with a little moist sand or moist paper towel. Leave them there for a period of time. Every plant is different but six to eight weeks should work. After that time, plant them. Success will be better if you can duplicate the conditions that you found them growing in in the wild. In the case of Cochise Beardtongue, that would involve shade during part of the day. Now, if you are going through all this waiting and effort, why not grow a few extras in some small pots? That way, you might have something to trade next time and not have to go through all this hassle.

As far as native evergreens like junipers or pines go, they are hard to find in nurseries and slow to grow from seed. Luckily, they are fairly easy to transplant. The whole key is to move them in winter after a wet spell. You could dig during the wet spell, but I have never been much for working in the rain. It might be possible to find a rancher who would be willing to let you dig up junipers on their property. That would be a win for all involved.

A couple more thoughts on seed collecting. In the wild, the odds of a seed growing into a mature plant are very small. Warren Jones, who was one of the pioneers in using native plants in landscaping, told me one time he thought maybe one seed in a million made it to a mature plant in the wild. I don't know if he meant that literally, or if that was his way of saying it doesn't happen very often. The point is, when you are harvesting seed for your own personal uses, don't take everything you find from every plant out there. There is a difference between harvesting and mining. You might not know that you made a difference, but the next critter that comes along possibly will. Also, know what you are collecting. There are plants out there (Natal Grass, some thistles) that are superficially attractive but do way more harm than good to the grasslands. Just because something is pretty doesn't mean it should be propagated.

Yellow Bluestem (AKA The Red Menace) invading

Invasives

It would be wrong in a book about grassland plant identification to not point out what species are native, introduced or invasive. Defining native is harder than it seems. The official, pencil-necked geek, botanical definition of native describes a plant that occurred in the given area before the arrival of that dastardly dude Columbus in 1492. Use that if you want, but I think Columbus has taken enough heat lately. I am not blaming him for the tumbleweed in my pasture. One thing I would like to clear up is that just because something is "native" doesn't make it superior. We all have driven through cities and seen misguided youths walking around the streets with their pants hanging down, all tatted up, blasting pumped up music while looking to score some crack. Well a lot of those folks are "natives" to their area, but I sure as heck don't think they are of a part of a healthy ecosystem. They are more like walking weeds. We are looking more towards beneficial natives. These are plants with characteristics that would provide food, shelter, shade etc. in a beneficial relationship to other species in that area. Beneficial natives do not invade an area and dominate it to the exclusion of other species. Species that do that would be considered invasive.

We all know climate changes through time, and that species come and go as a reaction to that change. What is different now, especially in the last hundred years, is that species are coming and going a lot faster than they used to. This is a direct result of man's domination of the landscape. Many times we have introduced species with the best of intentions, for purposes such as erosion control, improved grazing, or even aesthetic purposes. A lot of times, there are even very short term benefits to these introductions. Not all introduced species create problems. Fruit trees are introduced and most of us sure like them. Trouble starts when an introduced plant becomes invasive. Lehmann's Lovegrass is a classic example.

In the 1910s, a lot of land in southeastern Arizona was in bad shape due to a severe drought and mismanagement of livestock. Agricultural scientists went all over the world looking for species that would survive in our conditions, feed livestock, and hold the soil. One species they brought back from the savannahs in Africa has proved a little too successful. Lehmann's Lovegrass thrives in our conditions. It can flower twice a year, and can take hotter and dryer conditions than many of our native grass species. In the last quarter century it has spread and out-competed native species over many thousands of acres — and shows no real sign of stopping. Often, it is so successful it wipes out almost all of the native grass population. Why has it spread so rampantly? The main reason would be no natural predators. When Lehmann's was introduced, whatever keeps it in check in Africa wasn't. Also, most livestock prefer the more palatable native species. Cattle will nose through stands of Lehmann's to graze the native species. That greatly reduces their chances of producing seed. As a result, Lehmann's occurs in large monocultures with little plant diversity. High species diversity is one of the characteristics of a heathy grassland. Having a solid stand of Lehmann's limits the wildlife that occupies that area, greatly reduces the grazing potential, and changes the fire behavior, as it burns hotter than the natives.

The bottom line is that Lehmann's is so entrenched in the arid Southwest that it isn't going anywhere and folks that manage land are just going to have to learn to deal with it the best they can. Lehmann's is not the only invasive creating problems. There many other introduced species that create problems. High on today's list would be Tumbleweed, Johnsongrass, and my current least favorite Yellow Bluestem. It is hard to drive anywhere in the grasslands without seeing one of these species lining the road. The amount of time, effort, and money spent trying to control invasive species is huge and is, for the most part, a losing battle. Unfortunately, the cost of doing nothing might prove greater in terms of grazing land lost or wildfires carried by these species. Think before you seed.

How to Identify a Plant

The first step in identifying an unknown plant is to take a good look at it. (Hopefully, you have already paid for this book before you are privy to such insightful knowledge). Then, you might want to ask a series of questions to narrow down the choices. Is it a grass or "grass-like"? Does it have stems, and if so, are they woody or herbaceous? If it is woody, what does the bark look like? Before you grabbed it, did you notice any thorns? How about after you grabbed it? Most important is to check for a flower. Historically, all classification was based on floral characteristics. This explains why plants that have similar looking leaves, like a native walnut *(Juglans arizonica)* and Tree of Heaven *(Ailanthus altissima)* are not closely related, but a garden pea *(Pisum sativum)* and a mesquite *(Prosopis velutina)* are. If there is a flower, it is good to note how many petals and what their arrangement is.

Be aware of where it is growing. Is it in full sun or shade, slope or flat, and what did the soil look like where it was growing? If a plant that looks like Piñon Rice Grass is growing in the full sun on a western-facing slope, it probably isn't. I am not sure what it might be, but Piñon Rice Grass almost always grows in shade conditions. How much moisture is held in the area where it is growing? Deergrass, Giant Sacaton, and Seepwillows are rarely found in places that don't hold some extra moisture. Soil types can also be a help in identification. The plants growing in alkaline dirt will be quite different than plants growing in a red volcanic soil, even if the elevation, exposure, and slope are all the same.

Take advantage of all your senses. Does it have a unique smell or feel? Crush some leaves. Several plants, like Fetid Marigold or Sonoran Jasmine, could be easily identified with your eyes closed only by their smell. Some folks I work with like to taste plants to help figure out what they are. Many of the places I work have been recently grazed by cattle. I believe I will pass on tasting plants that large livestock has recently passed over.

One of the last things I do to identify a plant is try to yank it out of the ground. If it comes out easily, it is probably an annual species. The root system on an annual plant is usually smaller and weaker than a perennial plant. An annual species is like a rock star. It germinates easily, grows quickly, goes to seed and then dies in less than a year. Many of the species we consider weeds, like Tumbleweed, Pigweed, or Sandbur are annuals. Perennials take their time to complete their life cycles. They tend to live at least several years or more and may take years to bear seed. Perennials will have a more developed and fibrous system. If you can't pull the plant out with minimum of effort, leave it alone. It is probably a perennial. Healthy grasslands ideally should contain a mix, but be composed of mostly perennials. Remember though, anything that holds soil has some benefit.

Of course, we are dealing with living things, so not everything is cut and dried. There are long-lived annuals, short-lived perennials, and biennials. A perennial that has just sprouted will not have a well-developed or fibrous root system, and some plants, like Sensitive Partridge Pea, might be annual in some areas but perennials in other locations. But heck, we are having fun identifying grassland plants, so we are just not going to worry about any of that.

Now let's put all this "insightful knowledge" to the test.

This plant was growing in sandy soils and is grass-like. It came out of the ground very easily and has a weak root system. That makes it an annual. It has a very distinctive spiny bur as a seed. That would make it Sandbur. Identification made easy.

Some Almost Final Thoughts

This book was put together to be the kind of guide I wish I would have had when starting out. I have tried to avoid technical jargon in order to promote clarity. Upon reviewing the over 290 species, I was struck by how many of them only occur in the border states of Arizona, New Mexico, and Texas. Our unique conditions make for unique flora. Many of our flowers are beautiful but not large. To appreciate many of them, you have to get down on your hands and knees and look at them closely. That's OK, putting out a little effort is a good thing. We are the land of wind and water. At all times, no matter what you are looking at, it is impossible to overstate the importance of water to grasslands. Understand water and you will understand not just the grasslands but all of the Southwest.

Grasses

Grasses provide food and shelter to a variety of wildlife and livestock. They hold soil and prevent erosion better than any other plant group. This affects everything from plant composition to water quality. Almost all our grasses are considered 'warm season' species. They will grow in the summer when the ground temperature has warmed up and they have gotten some moisture. As you can tell by the photo dates, they flower in the late summer or fall. If two dates are listed, the first is for the big photo. During winter, no matter how much moisture falls, they remain dormant.

Identifying grass is all about the seed and seed heads. Though it is possible to identify grass based on vegetative characteristics it is hard and way above our pay grade. If a grass you were wondering about is not flowering, come back later when it is and you can figure it out then.

One more note before we get to the list of species. The size of a grass at flowering is very dependent on the amount of moisture it has received in the growing season. In a good year Sideoats Grama can grow almost 4' tall. In a droughty year it might flower, if at all, at less than 1'. For that reason, we aren't going to give a specific height for each species, but will instead group them in general categories according to the size they could be in a normal year (if we ever have a normal year).

Size Categories:
- Small: Less than 1'
- Medium: 1' to 3'
- Large: 3' to 5'
- XLarge: 5' and above

GRASSES

Bermudagrass
Cynodon dactylon

Small, introduced invasive, perennial

Bermuda makes a turf and reproduces from seed, underground roots, and trailing stems. Most livestock really like it. You will find Bermuda growing along many riparian banks, even miles away from civilization. 8/6/15

2

Beardgrasses
Bothriochloa

Cane Beardgrass
(Cane Bluestem)
Bothriochloa barbinodis

3

Large, native, perennial

Cane Beardgrass is a coarse grass, which often has a reddish tint to the leaves at the base. You can identify it by the tuft of hair at the nodes (joints of the stem). Try chewing on a seed. It reminds most folks of a slight berry taste. 10/27/13

Yellow Bluestem
(The Red Menace*)
Bothriochloa ischaemum

Medium, introduced invasive, perennial

4

Yellow Bluestem's flowers are purplish-red and look like fingers spreading outward from the stem. Stems and leaves turn pale yellow after flowering. This is a horrible plant that has shown the potential to change the grasslands more than any other grass species since Lehmann Lovegrass was introduced. Livestock don't seem to touch it in any phase of growth. (*I made up this appropriate common name because it fit so well.) 8/27/14

Bigflowered Tridens
(Shortleaf Woolygrass)
Erioneuron avenaceum

Medium, native, perennial

Bigflowered Tridens stands out because of its wooly seed head. It grows on limey soils. This plant used to be in the *Tridens* genus. 9/24/15 *(Leatherweed on left)*

5

Bristlegrasses
Setaria

Bristlegrasses all have bristles radiating out from the seed head.

6

Annual Bristlegrasses
Setaria grisebachii

Medium, native, annual

Annual Bristlegrass grows in shaded situations.
The leaves often are purple. It has a sparse
seed head. 10/24/15

Plains Bristlegrass
Setaria vulpiseta

Medium, native, perennial

The seed head on Plains Bristlegrass looks like something you might feed a parakeet. The leaves and stems cure to an amber color. Plains Bristlegrass is often found at the base of Mesquite trees or other shrubs. 8/28/13

7

Grasses

Buffelgrass
Pennisetum ciliare

Medium, introduced invasive, perennial

Many low desert areas are currently threatened by Buffelgrass, because of its ability to carry fire and outcompete native species. In the grasslands, it will probably just become one more in a list of not-so-desirable occupants. 9/22/15

8

Burrograss
Scleropogon brevifolius

Small, native, perennial

Burrograss is usually found on clay flats. It is an unusual grass in that male and female flowers are found on separate plants. The long seed needles get embedded in dried cracks in the soil in order to plant themselves. 9/24/15

9

Crabgrasses
Digitaria

Crabgrasses have a bad family name. Fortunately, not all of them are pesky or invasive.

Arizona Cottontop
Digitaria californica

Medium, native, perennial

Arizona Cottontop's seed heads are clustered together and resemble cotton from a distance. This is a good plant for livestock. 8/13/15

Hairy Crabgrass
(Giant Hairy Crabgrass)
Digitaria sanguinalis

Medium, introduced, annual

Hairy Crabgrass grows 1' to 2' wide and can spread wider than that, as the sprawling stems root at the nodes. It often shows up as an unwanted visitor in gardens or planter beds. The species name *sanguinalis* means red fingers and refers to the spreading seed heads. The common name sounds like it should be a villain in an old Western movie. 8/29/15

Fall Witchgrass
Digitaria cognata

Small/medium, native, perennial

Fall Witchgrass has a sparse, spreading flower stalk that can be hard to spot, but has a pinkish tinge. This stalk resembles a poor version of Plains Lovegrass. The best way to identify this plant is by its leaves. One side is smooth and the other is serrated. A little magnification helps to see this. 9/4/15

12

Crimson Bluestem
Schizachyrium sanguineum

Medium/large, native, perennial

Crimson Bluestem grows in a very upright form. Patches of it make beautiful fall color and it creates excellent habitat for ground birds. Highly recommended for home landscapes. Texas Bluestem is closely related and looks very similar. 8/24/15

13

Crinkle-Awn
(Spiked Crinkle-awn)
Trachypogon spicatus

Medium, native, perennial

14

Crinkle-Awn is a coarse grass with little forage value after initial growth. The seed head kind of resembles a mutant barley seed structure. Parts of the base of the plant turn reddish upon curing in the fall. Often seen with Wooly Bunchgrass. 10/14/15

Curly Mesquite
Hilaria belangeri

Small, native, perennial

Curly Mesquite is a common, shallow rooted, sod grass-forming plant. It reproduces by sending out runners (stolons) that root and form new plants. Seed stalks have a zigzag pattern at the top. You can identify this plant by slowly running your hand through a patch and seeing if you get caught by the runners. Make sure there is nothing you don't want to grab before you try that approach. 8/6/15

Dropseeds
Sporobolus

16

Giant Sacaton
(Big Sacaton)
Sporobolus wrightii

Xlarge, native, perennial

Giant Sacaton lives up to its name and can get
over 8' tall. It grows mainly in seasonally flooded
bottomlands. Because of its dense growth, it could
be useful as a screen or wind break. Many former
Sacaton bottoms were plowed up by pioneer
farmers to plant their crops. 11/2/13, 8/13/15

Sand Dropseed
Sporobolus cryptandrus

Medium, native, perennial

Sand Dropseed is unique in the way its seedpods are held in their sheath close to the stem before they ripen. These seeds are tiny with over 5 million to the pound. Sand Dropseed likes, but doesn't need, sandy or silty soils. 8/13/15

17

Feather Finger Grass
Chloris virgata

Small/medium, introduced, annual

A weedy plant that is common in disturbed areas. It is called Feather Finger because the seed structures radiating out from the stem look like fingers when open. 8/13/15

Fluffgrass
(Low Woolly Grass)
Dasyochloa pulchella

Small, native, perennial

Fluffgrass is a low growing plant that is found mainly on alkaline soils. The seed heads are covered with what looks like fluff. You will see Fluffgrass growing on harsh sites where not many other species of grass can make it. 8/13/15

19

Grama Grasses
Bouteloua

The Grama Grass family is the royal family of the grasslands. Most are desirable forage, attractive to look at, and an abundance of them can indicate a healthy range. Some are a food source for butterflies. Gramas grow over a wide variety of conditions.

Black Grama
Bouteloua eriopoda

Medium, native, perennial

Black Grama grows as a many-stemmed plant. The stems have multiple segments, (nodes) which are slightly hairy. When these stems touch ground they can root and form sod. The seed heads are thinner than Blue or Hairy Grama. Black Grama is often found on alkaline sites. 8/13/15

Blue Grama
Bouteloua gracilis

Medium, native, perennial

Blue Grama seed heads, often called flags, resemble arching caterpillars. Usually there are three or less per stem. Blue Grama really likes silty or loamy bottomlands, and can be very sod forming. It is an attractive plant and has been mixed with Buffalograss to use as a low water use lawn. It is excellent for livestock grazing and erosion control. Blue Grama truly is the Queen of the Grasslands. 9/21/13, 11/2/13

Hairy Grama
Bouteloua hirsuta

Small/ medium, native, perennial

The Hairy Grama seed head is similar to Blue Grama except it has a spikelet (point) on the end. It can grow in harsher and rockier conditions than Blue Grama. 10/18/13

22

Needle Grama
Bouteloua aristidoides

Small, native, annual

Needle Grama is a small annual up to about 8". The seed heads tend to grow on one side of the stem and are needle sharp. This can be one of the major sock-stickers that hikers in the grasslands are all too familiar with. It tolerates very hot dry conditions. 8/13/15

23

Purple Grama
Bouteloua radicosa

Small/medium, native, perennial

Purple Grama looks a lot like Sprucetop Grama.
The seed heads are a little longer and can appear
purple when maturing. When the leaves dry in the
fall they make a coarse mat that resembles wood
shavings at the base of the plant. 9/28/13, 8/29/15

Rothrock Grama
Bouteloua rothrockii

Medium, native, perennial

Although Rothrock Grama has a seed head similar to a small Blue Grama, it has many more of them per stalk than Blue. It often has eight to ten seed heads per stalk. Rothrock seeds turn reddish when maturing. It is a fairly short-lived perennial and a good pioneer species. 8/13/15

25

Sideoats Grama
Bouteloua curtipendula

Medium, native, perennial

Sideoats Grama is an upright growing plant. It is found in wide variety of conditions and is very common. When the seeds fall the tip of the seed stalk is left with a slight zigzag pattern at the tip. Even though it is called Sideoats, the seeds can grow on either one side or both sides of the stem. 8/2/15, 11/2/13

26

Slender Grama
Bouteloua repens

Small, native, perennial

Slender Gramas is another Sprucetop Grama look-alike. The easiest way to tell the difference is that Sprucetop seed heads have tiny hairs on them (pubescent) and Slender Grama is hairless. 8/26/15

27

Sprucetop Grama
Bouteloua chondrosioides

Small, native, perennial

Sprucetop Grama is often found with Curley Mesquite or other Sprucetop varieties like Purple or Slender Grama. The seeds are covered with small hairs. When the seeds drop, the top of the seed stem has a slight back and forth wave to it. Don't fret if you can't tell the different Sprucetop types (Sprucetop, Purple, Slender) apart.
They all have pretty much the same aesthetic, erosion control, and forage values to them.
8/16/14, 10/24/13

28

Johnsongrass
Sorghum halepense

Xlarge, introduced invasive, perennial

Johnsongrass is an aggressive invasive species that spreads by seed and underground roots. It prefers places that receive extra moisture, like the banks of washes, riparian areas, or even roadsides. Johnsongrass was the target species in the development of Roundup. 8/2/15

29

Lovegrasses
Eragrostris

Lovegrasses are all of the genus Eragrostis, which of course is named in honor of Eros, the god of love. I ask you now, who amongst us can gaze at these Lovegrass specimens and not feel a warm stirring deep in the loins? However, before you are tempted to give in and spread Eragrostis seed all over your private property, remember that all grasses of love are not good. The genus of Love contains some of the most invasive plants to be ever introduced into the grasslands. Many were brought in desperation and with good intentions, but once populations were established, they have altered the plant composition of the grasslands forever and probably not for the better. Maybe there is a lesson there – about messing with exotic flora… and love. All plants in the Lovegrass family have a seed head that is actually made up of many smaller seeds packed in together.

Stinkgrass

African Lovegrass
Eragrostis echinochloidea

Medium, introduced invasive, perennial

African Lovegrass is native to South Africa. Like many invasive species, it outcompetes and replaces more diverse native species. It appears to be moving higher in elevation. 8/26/15

31

Boer's Lovegrass
Eragrostis curvula var. conferta

Medium, introduced invasive, perennial

This coarse-looking plant can form large colonies, outcompeting native grasses. The seed heads resemble Lehmann Lovegrass but are much more robust. 9/4/15

Lehmanns left, Boers right

Lehmann Lovegrass
Eragrostis lehmanniana

Medium, introduced invasive, perennial

Lehmann Lovegrass is the poster child for introduced species gone wild. It has replaced tens of thousands of acres of native grasses. After the growing season, its bright green cures to a yellowish color that is easily recognized from a distance. Livestock and most wildlife will only graze it when it first greens up. On the positive side, it does a very good job of holding soil in place. 11/29/15

33

Plains Lovegrass
Eragrostis intermedia

Medium, native, perennial

Plains Lovegrass is one of the first native grasses to green up in the spring and one of the last to go dormant in the fall. The seed stalks look like a pink mist hovering over the plant in autumn. Livestock and wildlife love this plant. 8/6/15

34

Stinkgrass
Eragrostis cilianensis

Small/medium, introduced, annual

Stinkgrass has a large seed head compared to most of the Lovegrass family. It is very common in disturbed areas. 11/2/13

35

Weeping Lovegrass
Eragrostis curvula

Medium/large, introduced invasive, perennial

Weeping Lovegrass, another native of South Africa, is a thick deep green grass that likes a little extra moisture. The leaves are thin, almost wiry. It is often found on the sides of roads or in draws. Both the leaves and flower stalks weep when mature. It was often planted by government agencies on roadsides for erosion control. 8/6/15

Wilman Lovegrass
(Trilobite Grass*)
Eragrostis superba

Medium, introduced, perennial

Wilman Lovegrass has a large seed head that stands well above the plant. It is another native of South Africa. Close visual inspection of the seed head shows that it looks like a fossil trilobite, hence the uncommon common name of Trilobite Grass. (*Made up by the author) 8/6/15

37

Muhlys
Muhlenbergia

Muhlys are a large and very diverse group of related grasses that often seem to have nothing in common. What make them related is that they all have a small whisker (awn) that comes out of the individual seed. Sometimes you have to look closely to see it.

Bull Muhly in flower

Arizona Muhly
Muhlenbergia arizonica

Small, native, perennial

The leaves on Arizona Muhly look like a poor Bermudagrass. The flowers look like anemic Plains Lovegrass. Often you see this grass in small patches. Creeping Muhly (AKA Aparejo Grass) looks similar to Arizona Muhly but doesn't get the flower structure. 9/4/15

39

Bull Muhly
Muhlenbergia emersleyi

Medium to large, native, perennial

Bull Muhly is a robust grass found often on north-facing hillsides. It is very comfortable growing in shade and stays green year round. Bull Muhly makes an excellent landscape plant. 9/23/15

Bush Muhly
(Porter Muhly)
Muhlenbergia porteri

Medium, native, perennial

Bush Muhly is a very wispy plant that often grows at the base of shrubs or Mesquites. When in flower, it has an overall pink cast to it. It is often one of the few grass species that seems to thrive in shrub-encroached alkaline sites. 9/22/15 *(Silverleaf Nightshade surrounding plant)*

Deergrass
Muhlenbergia rigens

Medium/large, native, perennial

Deergrass is a coarse grass that grows where it can get extra water. It is usually found in canyon bottoms growing in stands. The seed head is narrow and never opens up. 11/2/13

42

Delicate Muhly
Muhlenbergia fragilis

Small, native, annual

Delicate Muhly is a small airy grass that you might not notice as a solitary plant. However, when you see a mass of them grouped together on a cool fall morning, they look like a light pink mist covering the ground. 11/16/13

43

Natalgrass

(Rose Natal Grass)

Melinis repens

Medium, introduced invasive, perennial

Natalgrass is a very pretty grass making way into the grasslands. Unfortunately, it is invasive and has already taken over many slopes, replacing the native species. The color of the flower can range from almost pure white to a rose pink color. You might be tempted to take some seed home and plant it. Don't. 8/26/15

44

Nodding Brome
Bromus anomalus

Medium, native, perennial

Nodding Brome has a weeping growth form because of its large seed heads. Although listed as a cool season species by many sources, it flowers in sync with other warm season species in Southeastern Arizona. It is found in draws and canyon bottoms in the shade.
8/10/15, 11/2/13

45

Panic Grasses
Panicum

Panic Grasses are another group of grasses with a wide variety of appearances. What ties them together is the seeds, which are large (for grass seed anyway) and rounded. The name Panic comes from the Latin word *panis,* which means bread. This tells you some species of *panicum* were probably ground into flour. The grain millet is a Panic Grass.

Gould's Turkey

Bulb Panic
Panicum bulbosum

Large, native, perennial

Bulb Panic prefers slightly moist places and can tolerate heavy soils. It gets its name from the bulbs, which grow a few inches underground. Quail and other wildlife feed on them. 9/21/13

47

Hall's Panic
Panicum hallii

Small, native, perennial

Hall's Panic usually grows in alkaline soils. When the leaves cure, they curl up like wood shavings at the base. Often found with Blue Threeawn or Slim Tridens. 8/24/15

48

Vine Mesquite
Panicum obtusum

Small, native, perennial

Vine Mesquite often grows in thick patches. It sends out long runners early in the season whenever it gets any moisture. Because of this, it is an excellent binder of soils. The foliage is blue-green in color and the seeds are large, almost BB pellet size. Grazers appreciate Vine Mesquite. It can be hard to propagate from seed. 8/16/14

Witchgrass
Panicum capillare

Small, native, annual

Witchgrass likes disturbed areas. It is very adapted to a variety of conditions and can be found in all lower forty-eight states. 8/26/15

Piñon Ricegrass
Piptochaetium fimbriatum

Medium, native, perennial

Piñon Ricegrass is a very soft-looking grass that is found in shaded areas. You might want to bend over and pet it. It stays green all year. It would be useful in a landscape spots that have limited sun exposures. 8/29/15

Sand Bur
(Coastal Sandbur)
Cenchrus spinifex

Small/medium, native, annual

This is just a nasty plant that is easily identified (too easily) by its spiked barbed seed heads. They hurt going in and they hurt going out. This plant prefers sandy soil conditions. The best control is hand pulling as soon as you notice the seed heads forming. 8/24/15

Sprangletops
Leptochloa

The genus name comes from the Latin root words *lepta* (slender) and *chloa* (grass). Nice name, but they don't seem any more slender than most other species of grasses.

Annual Sprangletop
(Mucronate Sprangletop)
Leptochloa panicea

Medium, native, annual

Annual Sprangletop grows on disturbed soils, and in the case of this picture, a mud puddle. There are several other species of Annual Sprangletops that look similar to this one. 8/24/15 *(Feather Fingergrass in foreground)*

Green Sprangletop
Leptochloa dubia

Large, native, perennial

Green Sprangletop towers over many of the native species of grasses. It is best identified by its flower structure, which really resembles a very poor corn tassel. The leaf sheaths flatten out at the base. 9/28/13

54

Spike Pappusgrass
(Nineawn Pappusgrass)
Enneapogon desvauxii

Small, native, perennial

Spike Pappusgrass is a small plant that has a silvery seed head and likes limey soils. 9/28/13 *(Three Awn in front)*

55

Slim Tridens
Tridens muticus

Medium, native, perennial

Slim Tridens seeds have a purple tint to them before they ripen. The leaves are blue-green and turn reddish when curing. It likes alkaline soils. 9/4/15

Squirreltail
Elymus elymoides

Medium, native, perennial

Squirreltail is one of the few cool season grasses in the grasslands. It can germinate in late fall or early spring if there is moisture. This makes it stand out from all the warm season species. Oh yeah, it has a large bushy seed head, too. 4/12/15

Tanglehead
Heteropogon contortus

Medium/large, native, perennial

Tanglehead wins the blue ribbon for the most appropriately named grass in the grasslands. The seeds are dark colored and the leaves are a yellowish green. It often grows on rocky slopes. 8/25/15

Three Awns
Aristida

Threeawns are some of the most common and confusing of all grass groups. What bonds them together is that they all have three awns (bristles) coming off the lemma, which is the covering of the actual grass flower. Proper identification is often based on characteristics that require a degree of magnification to uncover. You shouldn't worry too much about separating them out, as they seem to hybridize and most function the same way in terms of erosion control and livestock grazing. I have seen people with very good identification skills moved to use inappropriate language when trying to separate out Threeawns.

Pronghorn Antelope at rest

Annual Threeawn
(Prairie Threeawn)
Aristida oligantha

Small, native, warm season annual

This sparse plant can be very common, especially in wet summers. It is often found growing in a ring around harvester ant nests. 9/28/15

Blue Threeawn
(Allred Blue Threeawn)
Aristida purpurea var. nealleyi

Medium, native, perennial

Blue Threeawn is distinctive for its combination of large awns and rounded leaves. It is usually found on alkaline sites. 8/24/15

61

Purple Threeawn
Aristida purpurea

Medium, native, perennial

Purple Threeawn is often seen growing along roadsides. It has long awns that are purple before they ripen. 8/13/15

Spidergrass
Aristida ternipes

Medium/large, native, perennial

Spidergrass is one of the more common Threeawns. It is an open and spreading plant. Spidergrass looks like it only has one awn. The other two are held in tight, but there really are three. If you see a grass that looks just like Spidergrass and has all three awns showing, that is probably a closely related variety, Mesa Threeawn. 9/28/13

63

Tobosa
Pleuraphis mutica

Medium, native, perennial

Tobosa is usually found in low swales, which hold moisture due to their clay and silt content. These sites are sometimes referred to as Tobosa flats. There it grows in large colonies where it is the dominant species. Tobosa is very important for soil stabilization and livestock grazing. 8/13/15

Wooly Bunchgrass
(Woolyspike Balsamscale)
Elionurus barbiculmis

Medium, native, perennial

Wooly Bunchgrass is a soft-looking yellowish-green grass that often is found on rocky slopes. The leaves appear to be rounded. If you see it when it is starting to flower, the pollen grains are a bright lemon yellow color. 8/25/15

65

Yellow Nutsedge
(Nutgrass)
Cyperus esculentus

Small, native/introduced, perennial

Technically, Yellow Nutsedge is not a grass, but it looks like one so it is going in this section. The leaves, like all sedges, have three sides. The flower resembles large moth antennae (if a moth had three antennae). If you dig this plant up, you will find small bulbs at the base of it. 8/6/15

Trees and Shrubs

A few years ago I was involved with the filming of a segment of a television show called "Backyard Habitat". This episode was on the grasslands. While patiently waiting for my segment on reseeding to be shot I listened to the hostess, obviously not chosen for her botanical knowledge, ask the show's naturalist "How come there is nothing out there?" (Camera pans to wide open rolling grasslands.) "There is nothing out there because there is nothing out there" responded the naturalist "but when we plant these trees and shrubs here there will be something out there."

I almost puked. I wanted to shout to them "Hey, those are grasses and forbs you are looking at, that is not 'nothing'. Just check places that get a break from the wind, or sites that hold a little moisture, or even valleys where the mesquites have begun to encroach on the grasslands and you would see lots of trees and shrubs." I didn't tell them that though. After all it was only a television crew and next week they would be in a different location maybe looking at the ocean coast or a wetlands. Me, I would still be in our grasslands probably sitting under an oak tree.

What is the difference between trees and shrubs? Most traditional definitions have to do with height and number of trunks. Shrubs are considered to be less than 10" tall and have multiples of trunks. Trees are taller and have a single or a couple of trunks. However, as we said before, grassland plants can't read. Manzanita can have a single basal trunk and get over 12' tall and mesquites can have multiple trunks and stay short. It does us no good to separate them. The important thing to remember is that the mature growth of both trees and shrubs is hard and woody, and you need a saw to cut it.

For each specimen listed we have given the common name that is used, other common names (if any), botanical name, maximum growth height, and the date the photo was taken. Also listed are other plants if they show up in the photo. This gives a feel for the plant associations you might find in the specific growing conditions.

Acacias

Acacias are a group of very hardy shrubs and small trees. To be completely botanically accurate, there are no more acacias in the Southwest. For once, this is not a result of climate change or habitat destruction. No — because of the Great Botanical Name Robbery of 2011, Acacias can only be found in Australia. All our plants have been reclassified to other genera, like Senegalia or Vachellia. That doesn't matter, because we are still going call them Acacias. I'll give up my Acacias when you pry my cold, thorn-covered fingers from their trunks.

Creosote & Whitethorn Acacia (left) at Sunrise

Catclaw Acacia
Senegalia greggi

Large shrub or small tree up to about 20'. The thorns curve back toward main trunk and the seedpods are distinctive. Often grows near washes or drainages. Flowers are fragrant and creamy white to yellow. 8/26/15

69

Whiteball Acacia

(Fern Acacia)

Acaciella angustissima

Shrub up to about 3' tall with reddish-brown stems. Grows with multiple stems. This is a friendly acacia with no thorns. 8/9/14 *(Sotol in background)*

70

Whitethorn Acacia
(Vicid Acacia)
Vachellia vernicosa

Very sparse large shrub (or small tree) that grows up to about 10' tall and 8' wide. It has an asymmetrical growth form and is often found in alkaline soils. Yellow flowers in the spring. This plant is closely related to another plant also called Whitethorn Acacia, (Vachellia constricta) which does not have the asymmetrical growth form.
9/4/15

71

Arizona Ash
Fraxinus velutina

A large deciduous tree that grows up to 40' tall and as wide. It turns a bright yellow in the fall. The bark is grayish and striated. Older trees are usually missing the lower branches. If you have the room and are looking for a fast growing shade tree, Arizona Ash is a good choice. 9/24/15

Arizona Walnut
(Nogal)
Juglans major

A large tree that grows up to 50' tall along washes and streambeds. The nuts have good flavor but very little meat. Squirrels sure like them. They are a lot of work to crack for not much payoff. The wood has been used in furniture and occasionally musical instruments. 8/9/15

Bee Bush
(Wright's Beebush)
Aloysia wrightii

Bee Bush is a sprawling shrub that flowers in the fall. Smells a little like oregano and attracts many interesting insects. Grows up to about 5' by 5'. 9/4/15

74

Border Piñon
(Piñon)
Pinus discolor

The Border Piñon can grow to almost 50' tall, but is usually much shorter. The leaves (needles) are in bunches of three. They are white striped. The nuts have good flavor but are much harder to crack open than the more northern growing Piñon. Many times, the nuts that you find left on the tree are empty, which shows squirrels are smarter than we are. Hope that is not a big surprise. 11/2/13 *(Arizona White Oak, Palmer Agave in background)*

Bouvardia
(Firecracker Bush)
Bouvardia ternifolia

Bouvardia is a spectacular shrub that can grow to 4' by 4'. It is a member of the Coffee family. The bright orange flowers attract hummingbirds and butterflies. Bouvardia likes to grow on rocky outcroppings. 8/2/13

Brickella
(California Brickellbush)
Brickellia californica

This plant grows anywhere from 2' to 6' tall and up to 9' wide. The flowers are irregular shaped. It can often be found on limey soils. 9/4/15

Burrobush
(Cheese Burrobush)
Hymenoclea monogyra

Burrobush is a scraggly shrub that grows to about 5' tall and 5' wide. Its natural habitat is the banks of dry washes. 8/13/15

78

Burroweed
(Jimmyweed)
Isocoma tenuisecta

Burroweed grows in a mound from 1' to 3' tall and as wide. The remains of the yellow flowers turn tan and stay on the plant all year. Burroweed is toxic to all livestock. 9/4/15

Canyon Grape
Vitis arizonica

A fast-growing climbing vine that, at times, can cover an entire tree. The grapes are small and very acidic, but birds like them. Leaves turn yellow in the fall. Canyon Grape has been used experimentally as rootstock for wine grapes, as it is resistant to Pierce's Disease, a serious problem in some wine growing areas. 6/9/15

80

Cliffrose
(Mexican Cliffrose, Sweet Cedar)
Purshia mexicana

Cliffrose grows up to 12' tall and is usually taller than wide. It is an indicator plant that tells you the site where it is growing has alkaline soils. The blossoms smell so sweet that it is possible to ID Cliffrose just by the scent while driving though a patch. It does help to have your windows down. 8/9/14, 4/14/15

Coralbean
Erythrina flabelliformis

Coralbean usually grows as a series of stems to about 4' or 5' tall. It has bright red flowers that appear before the heart-shaped leaves come out. It flowers in conjunction with the northward hummingbird migration in the spring. The seeds are bright red and poisonous. Coralbeans often grow on the south side of a hill in rocky outcroppings, which protect its frost sensitive underground tuber.
8/11/14, 6/28/13

82

Cottonwood
Populus fremontii

Cottonwoods get huge, up to 100', and like lots of water. They grow in riparian zones. The leaves turn yellow in the fall. Some (the author) believe catching a falling Cottonwood leaf brings good luck for the coming year. Cottonwoods can be propagated in the spring by placing a cut branch in soil that stays moist. 11/2/13

83

Creosote
(Greasewood)
Larrea tridentata

Creosote can grow to over 10', but is usually seen in the 5' to 6' range. The chemical produced in its leaves and by its roots can inhibit other plants from germinating around or under it. That and the ability to send out root sucker clones are reasons why it is often found in pure stands. Creosote stands can be ancient, with the oldest believed to be more than 11,000 years old. 9/22/15

Crucifixion Thorn
(Crown of Thorns)
Koeberlinia spinosa

Crucifixion Thorn can be a large shrub or small tree that tops out at about 15'. The small leaves drop once it gets hot in the spring and photosynthesis occurs in the green stems. This is a nasty looking plant – unless you really like thorns. 9/4/15

85

Desert Broom
Baccharis sarothroides

Desert Broom can grow to 8'. There are separate male and female plants, which bloom in late fall or winter. This plant is very deep rooted and hard to get rid of once established. Desert Broom is very successful in disturbed areas. 11/23/15

Desert Broom Male   *Desert Broom Female*

Desert Honeysuckle
Anisacanthus thurberi

Desert Honeysuckle is an upright shrub that usually grows about 5' tall along dry washes. Its orange to reddish flowers are in bloom during the hummingbird migrations, especially in the spring. It makes a good landscape plant. 4/20/14

Desert Willow
Chilopsis linearis

Desert Willow grows up to about 30' by 20' wide. The color of its flowers varies from light lavender to purple. They attract hummingbirds, butterflies and other pollinators. The leaves give off a light, sweet smell in spring. It is a top choice for landscaping. It should be noted that the nursery trade has bred cultivars specifically for flower color. While fun to look at these, cultivars don't supply the pollen necessary to attract or feed the flying wildlife. 8/6/15, 8/19/14

Fairyduster
(False Mesquite, Guajilla)
Calliandra eriophylla

Fairyduster grows up to 2' tall and as wide. It blooms after rain events and is a good pollinator plant and browse for livestock. Often found on rocky slopes. 9/22/15 *(Limestone rocks in background)*

89

Four Wing Saltbush
Atriplex canescens

Four Wing Saltbush grows to about 5' tall and as wide. There are separate male and female plants. The seeds have, well, four wings. This plant is found in a wide variety of sites and conditions and is very drought tolerant. 9/22/15

Golden Current
Ribes aureum

Golden Currents usually grow between 4' and 10' tall and are found in moist soils. It is an excellent plant for attracting wildlife, as the stems are browsed in the spring and the berries attract birds in late summer. If there are any berries left, you can make jam out of them. 3/1/15

91

Graythorn
Ziziphus obtusifolia

Graythorn grows to about 6' tall with many asymmetrical branches. It drops its leaves when stressed and has small flowers that are easily overlooked. This plant is well named. Thorns are at the end of the branches, which don't grow opposite of each other. 8/13/15

Hackberries

Hackberries (Celtis) are members of the Elm family.
There are two kinds of Hackberries in the grasslands.

Canyon Hackberry
Celtis reticulata

93

Canyon Hackberry is a deciduous tree that grows to about 30'. The leaves feel a bit like sandpaper. The bark is gray and often has many "warts" on it. This makes it easy to tell apart from other gray barked trees. Canyon Hackberry produces berries that the birds like. Because of the way its branches interweave, it also makes a good nesting tree.
10/1/15

Desert Hackberry
(Spiny Hackberry)
Celtis ehrenbergiana

Desert Hackberry is a gnarly, intertwined shrub that can grow to about 8' tall and 10' wide. The branches grow in a zigzag pattern. Because of its growth form, it is a good plant for sheltering wildlife. 11/23/15

Juniper

Junipers are evergreen, slow growing, very hardy trees. They make good firewood and fence posts. Juniper berries are eaten by a variety of wildlife. You often see consumed berries in the scat of coyotes, raccoons, bears, and skunks. In some situations they can become invasive.

Alligator Juniper
Juniperus deppeana

Alligator Juniper is a long-lived (sometimes over 500 years) evergreen tree that can reach heights of 50'. The leaves are usually blueish green, but the best identification characteristic is the bark, which looks like alligator skin.
10/6/13

One Seed Juniper
Juniperus monosperma

One Seed Juniper is an evergreen tree that can reach a height of 25'. Its leaves are usually an olive green color. The bark is gray-brown, and appears long and stringy. 11/23/15 *(Ocotillo in front)*

Arizona Madrone
Arbutus arizonica

Arizona Madrone is a leafy evergreen tree that can grow to about 40' in the right conditions. It is best known for its reddish bark, which occurs on the branch ends. Older bark is checked and gray in color. Arizona Madrone is uncommon, but can be found in moist canyons. It has white flowers and blooms in summer months. 5/13/14

Point Leaf Manzanita
Arctostaphylos pungens

This Manzanita is best known for its red bark.
It can grow to 12' tall and often makes hard
to penetrate thickets. It is an evergreen shrub
that flowers in late winter. The berries are prized
by wildlife. Manzanita wood burns hot and
is good for smoking meats and fish. 2/23/14
(Beargrass in front, One Seed Juniper in back)

Mariola
Parthenium incanum

Mariola is a gray-green plant with deeply lobed leaves that grows to about 3'. It prefers limey soils and slopes. Mariola contains a small amount of rubber. It has small white flowers in summer to fall. 9/4/15

100

Mesquite

Mesquites are the most common trees in the grasslands. A lot of folks believe that once the mesquites leaf out, there will be no more frosts that year. Mesquite beans are excellent food for wildlife and cattle. The wood is excellent for burning and cooking. It is also used for furniture and fence posts. Mesquite leaves are the poster child of arid adaption, as they look like a 'normal' leaf that has had all the unnecessary portions removed.

Texas Honey Mesquite
Prosopis glandulosa

Texas Honey Mesquite is a spreading deciduous tree that can grow to about 25'. It has larger leaves than the Velvet Mesquite, and kind of a weeping growth habit. It is often found by roadsides or train tracks. 11/2/13

Velvet Mesquite left
Texas Honey Mesquite right

Velvet Mesquite
Prosopis velutina

Velvet Mesquite grows as a large shrub
or tree to over 30'. Some would say that it
does *too* well here, as it can become invasive
and will outcompete and replace the
native grass population. 8/13/15

101

Mexican Elderberry
(Blue Elderberry)
Sambucus nigra

Mexican Elderberry can grow to about 30' and almost that wide. It greens up very early in late winter and can drop leaves if it is drought stressed. The berries ripen in early summer and are good for jams and attracting wildlife. Mexican Elderberry can be propagated from cuttings. 8/26/15

Mimosas

Mimosas are great shrubs… if you like thorns.

Catclaw Mimosa
(Wait-a-Minute Bush)
Mimosa aculeaticarpa var biuncifera

Catclaw Mimosa grows to about 4' tall and is often wider than it is high. It flowers with a ball shaped white bloom in the summer. The key to identifying it is the curved thorns that point downward. This plant often grows in thick patches that are ready to slash clothes and flesh when one tries to pass through them. 11/2/13

Velvetpod Mimosa
Mimosa dysocarpa

Velvetpod Mimosa grows to 4'. It flowers with a spectacular show of vibrant pink and white flowers in the summer. Because of this showy display, some folks might want to plant it in their yards. That might be regretted later because of its other obvious feature – its many thorns. These thorns point straight out, which make it possible to tell apart from Catclaw Mimosa. 8/8/14 *(Sotol on right)*

104

Mormon Tea
(Ephedra)
Ephedra trifurca

Mormon Tea is a leafless sprawling shrub that can grow over 5' tall and get much wider. It is a very old plant with fossil history dating back over 200 million years. A tea brewed from this plant will contain ephedra, a stimulant. 9/22/15

Native Cotton
(Thurber's Cotton)
Gossypium thurberi

Native Cotton grows, often by roadsides, to a height of about 10'. It flowers with white blossom late in the summer or early fall. It makes a great landscape plant for those who appreciate fall color. 9/22/15

Oaks

Oaks are the dominant trees of the upper reaches of the grasslands. Most are semi-deciduous and have small leathery leaves that help conserve water loss. Native oaks are wind pollinated and drop their leaves (get naked) in the spring to facilitate pollination. In times of drought, oaks drop their leaves too.

Oak leaves are helpful for identification, but even on a single tree, there is often a lot of variation in leaf form. Many oaks are said to hybridize, which only makes identification by foliage more difficult. All species of oak are great for firewood and smoking meats. Some larger trees are used for furniture.

Hooded Oriole on flowering Emory Oak

Arizona White Oak
Quercus arizonica

Arizona White Oak can grow over 50' tall and is often found in canyon bottoms. Leaves are rounded but not smooth on the edges. The best way to ID Arizona White Oak is by the long striated light gray bark. The acorns usually start to fall around the start of the school year (August to September). 8/6/2015

108

Emory Oak
(Black Oak, Blackjack Oak)
Quercus emoryi

Emory Oaks grow slowly to 50' tall. The leaves are a solid green and Holly shaped. The bark is dark, almost black, and checked. The acorns of the Emory Oak are the best for eating and are prized by many species of wildlife. They usually start to ripen and fall with the start of summer rains (July). 8/7/2015

109

Mexican Blue Oak
Quercus oblongifolia

Mexican Blue Oak is a very drought tolerant tree, growing to about 25' tall. The bark is gray and separated into bark platelets. The best way to ID Mexican Blue Oak is by the leaves, which are blueish, oblong-shaped and have smooth edges. The acorns for this tree usually are ready in late fall (November to December). Mexican Blue Oak makes a really nice, if slow growing, landscape tree. 8/6/2015

Poison Ivy
(Western Poison Ivy)
Toxicodendron rydbergii

Poison Ivy is found in moist canyons and grows to about 3'. Although it is a member of the Cashew family, you sure wouldn't want to get it on your nuts or trail mix, as all parts of the plant are poisonous. If you see a plant that looks like Poison Ivy, it probably is, so don't touch it. Sure has nice fall color though. 11/2/13

111

Rabbitbrush
(Rubber Rabbitbrush)
Ericameria nauseosa

Rabbitbrush is a common plant along sandy wash bottoms. It can grow to about 6' and often makes thick stands. Rabbitbrush is one of the very last shrubs to flower, so it attracts a herd of pollinators – kind of like being the only guy or gal at a dance. Planting it extends the fall blooming season. It prefers sandy soils. 11/2/13 *(Painted Lady Butterfly)*

Sandpaper Bush
(Rio Grande Saddlebush)
Mortonia scabrella

Sandpaper Bush grows to about 6' tall. The leaves resemble a round braid going up the stems. The flowers are white and bloom happens after rains. The roots are orangeish in color. Sandpaper Bush is found in alkaline soils and often grows in solid patches. 9/4/15

113

Seepwillow
(Mulefat)
Baccharis salicifolia

Seepwillow can grow to about 8'. It is almost always found in or around washes or other moist areas. It draws many pollinators. (For all you preppers, it is a sought-after wood that is used in hand drills for fire starting.) 8/6/15

Senecio
(Threadleaf Ragwort)
Senecio flaccidus

Senecio is a gray-green shrub that grows, mainly along dry washes, to a height of about 5'. Senecio looks similar to Rabbitbrush, but its leaves are fleshier and more succulent looking. Senecio's flowering season starts in the spring and can continue all summer, while Rabbitbrush flowers very late in the fall. Senecio contains alkaloids that can be toxic to livestock, causing liver damage.
6/9/15

Silktassel
(Wright's Silktassel)
Garrya wrightii

Silktassel is a densely growing shrub that can get to about 10'. Often it grows as a understory plant beneath oaks. Its purple berries attract birds. Some folks refer to Silktassel as Green Manzanita. I have pretty low standards for common names, but that is a bad one. The two are easy to tell apart, as Silktassel has gray bark, not red. 10/24/13
(Emory Oak in Background)

Soapberry
(Western Soapberry)
Sapindus saponaria var. drummondii

Soapberry can get 30' tall but is usually much less. It often grows as a cluster of trunks. Soapberry turns yellow in the fall. The berries are poisonous (saponin) but have been used to make soap in the early days. 10/3/15 *(Three Leaf Sumac and Alligator Juniper in background)*

Spreading Ratany
(Trailing Krameria)
Krameria lanceolata

Spreading Ratany is a small plant, less than 1' tall with a pretty flower. It is worth getting down on your hands and knees to check it out. There are a couple of other Ratanys in the grasslands and they all have interesting flowers. 4/13/14

Sumacs

Sumacs *(Rhus)* are an important group of berry-producing shrubs that are an important food source for birds and other wildlife. Sumacs' cover makes for good small animal shelter. If you choose to plant one, make sure you let it dry out between watering. As a rule, most *Rhus* don't like to be constantly moist.

Evergreen Sumac
Rhus virens

Evergreen Sumac grows to about 8' tall and 10' wide. It flowers with a creamy white flower in the spring. Its leaves, which it holds all year, are glossy and deep green. 9/4/15

Littleleaf Sumac
Rhus microphylla

Littleleaf Sumac grows to about 6' tall. It definitely prefers to grow in alkaline soils. The white flowers come out before the leaves in the spring. 9/24/15

Threeleaf Sumac
(Skunkbush)
Rhus trilobata

Threeleaf Sumac can get to about 6' tall. It likes the growing conditions under other large vegetation, such as oaks. Leaves can turn an attractive red color in the fall before they drop. 10/11/13

Arizona Sycamore
Platanus wrightii

Arizona Sycamores get huge, almost 80' tall. With their light colored patchy bark and large leaves, no other tree looks like them. Arizona Sycamore is only found in gravely moist canyon bottoms. Compared to Sycamores from other regions, the leaves are more deeply indented, leaving less leaf surface. This is probably a water conserving strategy. Many Sycamores, especially planted in urban areas, get leaves that look scorched during the hot, dry seasons. This is not a great choice for home landscapes. 10/12/13

Tree of Heaven
(Tree from Hell)
Ailanthus altissima

123

The Tree of Heaven has been called the most invasive tree in America. It can grow to a height of about 25' or more. Tree of Heaven produces chemicals in its leaves and roots that inhibit other species from growing around it. It might be a little hard to distinguish it from Arizona Black Walnut. Look at the end of the new growth. The Tree of Heaven has fuzzy reddish tips. Also, the Tree of Heaven stinks, literally. 8/6/15

Trixis
(American Threefold)
Trixis californica

Trixis grows about 3' by 3'. A native perennial, it likes rocky slopes. It blooms in the spring and then again in response to summer rains. 4/9/15

Wolfberry
(Water Jacket)
Lycium andersonii

There are several Wolfberries that grow in the grasslands. A native perennial, generally they get about 6' tall. The berries are very nutritious and the shrubs are often visited by pollinators.
9/22/15 *(Palmers Metalmark Butterfly)*

Yerba de Pasmo
Baccharis pteronioides

Yerba de Pasmo is a scraggly asymmetrical shrub, generally about 4'. It has male and female flowers on separate plants, which look different from each other. The leaves generally have teeth along their margins. Yerba de Pasmo has been used for a host of veterinary purposes. A native perennial. 8/24/15

Cacti and Succulents

Mixed in the grasslands vegetation are plants that are often associated more with the low deserts, cacti and succulents. A succulent is any plant that uses its leaves, stems, or root system for long term moisture storage, a great survival adaptation in arid areas. To achieve cactus status you have to have certain floral parts common to the cactus family (Cactaceae). This makes all cactus succulents, but not all succulents are cactus. Cacti only occur naturally in the western hemisphere (North and South America). If you see something that looks like a cactus in other parts of the world it has either been imported (who wouldn't want cactus?) or it is not really a cactus.

What makes the cacti and succulents of the grasslands unique is their ability to tolerate cold. Many winter nights are below freezing in the grasslands and periodically you can see temperatures close to zero. These conditions would turn most columnar cacti, like saguaros, into a pool of green mush. Often the cacti and succulents in the grasslands are found on south or west facing slopes or in rocky outcroppings.

In this section we have included the common name, official common name, botanical name, and some basic information for each plant.

Agaves

Agaves are some of the most interesting plants in the grasslands. They can survive extreme heat and drought, and are mistakenly called 'Century Plants.' Most live for ten to fifteen years and then flower and die. That might seem like a long time, but is nowhere near a century. Agave flowers are an important source of food for hummingbirds, some bats, bees, and butterflies. Of course, Agaves are an important food source for humans, too — as they provide us with tequila and bacanora (a local, homemade tequila-like beverage).

128

Female Broad-tailed Hummingbird seeks agave nectar

Huachuca Agave
Agave parryi

Huachuca Agaves can grow to over 3' in diameter. The leaves are short and squat compared to the size of the plant. They can reproduce by sending out root shoots that form pups. These pups are clones of the mother plant. This could result in a large patch of Huachuca Agaves that is genetically identical. Huachuca Agave is a great choice for planting in harsh conditions that are hard to water.

4/12/15, 6/29/15

129

Palmer Agave
Agave palmeri

Palmer Agave has long, thin leaves. The plant can be anywhere from pale green to blue-green in color. Cold can give them a purple tint. Palmer Agave's flowers are a major food source of several species of bats. The size of this plant is very dependent on growing conditions. Some will flower out at about 2' while others grow over 5' in diameter before flowering. 8/6/15, 11/3/13 *(Thistle and Side Oat Grama in picture)*

Shindagger
(Schott's Century Plant)
Agave schottii

Shindaggers can grow to about 18" by 18". Their flowers are lemon yellow on about a 6' stalk. They grow in colonies that often get quite large. Anyone who has ever tried to walk through one of these colonies knows why they are called Shindaggers.
11/23/15

131

Arizona Fishhook Cactus
Mammillaria grahamii

The Arizona Fishhook is a small solitary cactus that doesn't grow much more than 5" tall. The spines are curved like a fishhook. It flowers with a whitish to lavender flower in July. The fruits look like little red chilies and are referred to as *chilitos*. They are good to eat. As with many solitary cacti, if the growth tip is disturbed, they can form a cluster of heads. 9/22/15

Arizona Rainbow
Echinocereus rigidissimus

The Arizona Rainbow can grow to almost 14" but is usually seen in the 4" to 6" range. The bands of alternating white and pink spines make this cactus easy to identify. They like rocky well-drained hillsides. The Arizona Rainbow's flower occurs in late spring. Although quite showy, it lasts only a day. I believe this is a very useful life lesson, which should be taught to all people of reproductive age.
5/15/14

133

Barrel Cactus
(Compass Barrel)
Ferocactus wislizeni

134

Barrel Cactus can grow to over 5', but grassland specimens usually stay below 2'. They are heavily spined. Barrel Cactus bloom when it gets hot. The flowers are yellow to orangeish. Yellow fruit hangs on the plant for most of the year and is edible. It is a myth that you can drink water from a Barrel Cactus. The nasty pulp is bitter and will mess up your insides. Barrels can be handy in survival situations though, as they almost always lean toward the south. 4/20/14 *(Vermillion Flycatcher on Barrel)*

Beargrass
(Sacahuista)
Nolina microcarpa

Beargrass grows about 4' high and 4' wide. It has long, thin leaves that have small teeth on the sides. Do not run your hands up and down these leaves or you might bleed. This plant may not look like a succulent, but if you were to buzz cut all the leaves off, you would see a stem structure that resembles a tortoise shell. This is where the moisture is stored. Beargrass is very tolerant of alkaline conditions.
8/6/15

Beehive Cactus
(Spinystar)
Escobaria vivipara

The Beehive Cactus is a small, solitary cactus that grows to about 4" high. In area of high traffic, (cattle, illegals, deer) the growth tip can get disturbed, which causes the Beehive Cactus to form a cluster. Very attractive magenta flowers in early summer. 8/24/15

Mammillarias and Escobarias can look very similar. A good way to tell the difference is that Escobarias have a slit on each of the nipples that make up the plant. Mammillarias don't.

Cholla
Cylindropuntia sp.

There are several types of Cholla that grow in the grasslands. They all have long cylindrical branches. Most are known for having pieces that break off and stick in various parts of your anatomy. These pieces, if left undisturbed on the ground, can root in place. The plant pictured is Cane Cholla. 3/1/15 *(Cylindropuntia spinosior)*.

137

Chihuahuan Pineapple Cactus

(White Fishhook Cactus)

Echinomastus intertextus

Chihuahuan Pineapple Cactus grows about 6" tall. You can often find it hanging onto the ground by only a thin root or two. That could be an indication it doesn't like wet conditions. This cactus is the first to flower, with a creamy white blossom in the late winter. When I see this plant in bloom, it reminds me of all the projects I was going to do in the off-season that didn't get done. 8/24/15

Hedgehogs
Echinocereus sp.

Hedgehogs are short columnar cacti that grow in clusters up to 12" tall by 2' wide. Most have very attractive flowers that range in color from orange to hot magenta. The fruits on some varieties are edible and said to taste like strawberries. They work well in pots. *(Top photo: Pink Flowered Hedgehog – Echinocereus fasciculatus with yellow Bahia flowers. Bottom photo: Claretcup – Echinocereus triglochidiatus – has orange/red flower) 9/22/15, 4/27/14*

Heyder Pincushion
(Little Nipple Cactus)
Mammillaria heyderi

140

Heyder Pincushion swells up to about 2" tall after a rain. There is also a stem that grows several inches underground. It and its closely-related species are the only cactus that contain a sticky latex. When this plant dries out, it sinks close to ground level and gets covered with debris, making it hard to spot. The manly cowboy knife, used for scale in the picture, is 4.5" long. 10/5/15

Ocotillo
Fouquieria splendens

No description is necessary for Ocotillos. The picture says it all. No other plant even looks close to an Ocotillo. It produces leaves after moisture events. After a good summer rainy season comes to a close, the green leaves turn golden brown. That is what we call fall color in the grasslands. 5/11/13

141

Prickly Pear Cactus
Opuntia sp.

There are quite a few species of Prickly Pear Cactus in the grasslands. They all have disc-like pads that are much longer than they are thick. Newly growing pads are called nopales, and are edible as is the fruit when ripe. Most Prickly Pear have large spines that you can see and smaller spiny hairs call glochids. Contact with either type of spine is not fun, but the glochids can be particularly irritating. 9/4/15 *(Tulip Pricklypear – Opuntia phaeacantha)*

142

Sotol
(Desert Spoon)
Dasylirion wheeleri

Sotols can grow to about 4' by 4' wide. They have male and female flowers on separate plants and are very hardy. The edges on the leaves are hooked and will draw blood if you push against them. Plants usually only have one head, but clusters of individuals can grow in the same area. 11/3/13 *(Emory Oak in background)*

143

Yuccas

Yuccas have a unique story. All Yuccas flower with a stalk of white flowers. White reflects moonlight best. Nighttime is when their pollinator, the Yucca Moth, is active. The Yucca Moth lays eggs that develop in the Yucca seedpod. As the Yucca Moth's larvae hatch, they feed on some, but not all, of the yucca seed. This symbiotic relationship benefits both species. Most Yucca work well in landscape situations.

Banana Yucca
Yucca baccata

Banana Yucca has variable growth forms and heights. Often, you find it with many heads. Banana Yucca gets its name from the fruit it produces, which is banana-shaped. The leaves often have long filaments on the sides. 9/22/15

Mountain Yucca
(Schott's Yucca)
Yucca schottii

Mountain Yucca grows to about 10' tall and has smooth blue-green leaves. It is usually a single-headed plant when young, but can branch later. A good way to tell Mountain Yucca is by the red margins on the leaves. This is one of the few native succulents that is very tolerant of growing in the shade. 6/29/13

Soaptree Yucca
Yucca elata

Soaptree Yucca can grow to 20' but most are much shorter. The leaves are flexible and have white threads along the edges. Soaptree Yuccas have a long underground trunk. A 4' or 5' plant may have that much growing below the surface before you get to the root system. This makes them very hard to transplant. 11/2/13

Forbs

Forbs are the wild children of the grasslands. They contain some of the most loved (penstemons, poppies, culinary herbs) and despised (Pigweed, Tumbleweed, Locoweed) plants that grow there. Many are annuals and in a good year will blanket whole hillsides in color. In a drought you would not even know they exist as they wait as seeds for the right conditions to germinate and repeat the cycle. Some can remain viable 10 years or more.

What characterizes a forb is that its mature stem and trunk tissue is soft. If you can cut a mature plant trunk with a pair of kitchen scissors you are probably looking at a forb. In the description of each plant you will find the common name, the official common name if different, the botanical name, and the potential mature height. Also noted is whether the plant is native or introduced, and if the plant is annual or perennial. The date the photo was taken is listed, too. This can be important especially for identifying cool season species. If two dates are listed, the first is for the large photo.

The forbs are grouped by the flower color. I admit this is not a perfect system as flower colors can vary in a species or be influenced by exposure and soil type. Also, flowers change shades during the maturation process. Fresh flowers attract new pollinators. To make grouping by colors even more confusing, I am a man and it has been proven that men and women see colors differently. I apologize if my "lilac" is your "lavender" or your "saffron" is my "gold".

Antelope Horns
(Spider Milkweed)
Asclepias asperula

148

2', native, perennial

Antelope Horns bears a fragrant flower in the spring. It not only provides larval food for monarch caterpillars and pollen for adult monarchs, it also gives butterflies a toxic flavor when consumed that makes them less likely to be eaten by predators. 5/8/14

Bolivian Cilantro

(Yerba Porosa)

Porophyllum ruderale

18", native, warm season annual

Bolivian Cilantro is used in Mexican and South American cooking. The flower heads look like they should open up and be showy but never do. Small flower parts protrude out of the ends of these floral buds. Bolivian Cilantro could be cultivated commercially. 8/29/15

Cocklebur
(Rough Cocklebur)
Xanthium strumarium

150

3' x 3', native, warm season annual

Cocklebur is known for its seedpods, which are covered in hooked spines that catch on just about everything. It is one of the more disliked plants by ranchers. Not only does it have toxic properties when grazed, but the burs are a serious irritant to livestock, especially when under a saddle. 8/6/15

Dichondra
(New Mexico Ponysfoot)
Dichondra brachypoda

3", native, perennial

151

Dichondra grows in shaded conditions and makes a great ground cover. It reproduces by sending out runners that root. Some ambitious person could make a business out of growing it on a commercial scale. 9/24/15

Doveseed Croton

(Leatherweed)

Croton potsii

18", native, perennial

Doveseed Croton is fairly common in the grasslands. Its leaves, petalless flowers, and fruit all appear grayish-green. 8/13/15

Eryngo
(Wright's Eryngo)
Eryngium heterophyllum

3', native, perennial

Eryngo is a very unique-looking plant that resembles a thistle. Its silvery green flowers hold their shape and color for a long time. Because of this, they are used in dry flower arrangements. 8/6/15

Monsterwort
Parthenice mollis

6', native, warm season annual

Monsterwort really stands out in the grasslands because of its leaf size. It blooms after summer rains. Some folks are allergic to it. 8/26/15

154

Pigweed
(Carelessweed)
Amaranthus palmeri

6', native, warm season annual

155

Pigweed is a very fast-growing, very green plant that likes disturbed areas. Early in its life it is an edible food plant, but as it matures, especially if stressed, it can contain toxic levels of nitrates. Each plant can produce hundreds of thousands of seeds. Best control of Pigweed is to mow early and often. 8/13/15

Ragweed
(Weakleaf Bur Ragweed)
Ambrosia confertiflora

2', native, perennial

Ragweed is a very high pollen producing plant. It spreads by rhizomes and often makes patches in disturbed ground. 8/13/15

Tumbleweed

(Prickly Russian Thistle)

Salsola tragus

4'x4", introduced invasive, warm season annual

157

There is nothing romantic about tumbling tumbleweed. This plant is a noxious pest and can be toxic to livestock. Tumbleweed is usually found in disturbed areas, where it outcompetes the natives in reestablishment. It has two kinds of flowers, males and bisexuals. The best treatment for control is frequent mowing. 8/6/15

White Sage

(White Sagebrush)

Artemisia ludoviciana

3', native, perennial

White Sage often grows on rocky hillsides. Its gray color makes a nice contrast to other green plants in a landscape situation. 8/6/15

Beggarticks
Bidens sp.

2', native, warm season annual

The name *Bidens* means two teeth. If you look at a single seed, you will notice two 'teeth' sticking off the floral edge. There is an untrue rumor of a separate but related species in Arkansas called Unidens. Beggarticks is another species that will stick in socks and pants. 8/29/15

159

Clammy-weed
(Sandyseed Clammy-weed)
Polanisia dodecandra sp. trachysperma

160

2', native, warm season annual

Clammy-weed grows in sandy soils. The flowers are white with red stamens. The whole plant is sticky and attracts bees and butterflies. 8/26/15

Clematis
(Western White Clematis)
Clematis ligusticifolia

18', native, perennial

Clematis is a vine that grows in moist pockets. At times it can become woody. The seed's structure is showier than the flowers. 4/18/14, 6/23/14

161

Climbing Wartclub
Boerhavia scandens

Climbing Wartclub is a vining shrub that can usually be found growing under other trees. Mesquite is a favorite. It attracts a variety of insects. 8/13/15

162

Cooley's Bundleflower
Desmanthus cooleyi

1', native, perennial

Cooley's Bundleflower is very common and is found on a wide variety of sites and soil conditions. It flowers in the early summer with a white flower that turns pinkish as it matures. The stems have lengthwise lines on them. 8/29/15

163

Cudweed
(Wright's Cudweed)
Pseudognaphalium canescens

2', native, warm season, annual

164

Cudweed really stands out with its whitish-gray color. The plant smells like the spice cumin. It germinates in winter and, depending on the conditions, can be annual, biennial, or perennial. 8/24/15

Desert Zinnia
Zinnia acerosa

(1', native, perennial

Desert Zinnia grows as a compact mound.
It can bloom from spring to fall. It likes,
but is not limited to, limey soils. 9/22/15

165

Dwarf Stickpea
Calliandra humilis

6", native, perennial

Dwarf Stickpea is a small plant that resembles several other grassland species, such as Cooley's Bundleflower or Hog Potato. Its flowers are white, turning pink as they mature. Stickpea has wider leaves than the other, similar species. The seedpod is also diagnostic, as it is broader and has pronounced ridges around the edge. 8/24/15

Fleabane
Erigeron sp.

2', native, biannual

There are several types of Fleabane in the grasslands. Some trail, others are upright. Some can be annuals. They all have small, daisy like flowers. 8/10/15

167

Guara

(Scarlet Beeblossom)

Oenothera suffrutescens

2', native, perennial

168

There are several Guaras in the grasslands. Most have small, attractive flowers and draw pollinating moths. These flowers can turn from white to scarlet in a day. Guaras work well in landscape situations. 4/13/14

Hairy Fournwort
Tetramerium nervosum

1', native, perennial

This plant needed to be included, if only for its name. Hairy Fournwort is very unique-looking. It can bloom from spring through fall. The uppermost petal has a dash of purple in the center. 8/26/15

169

Horehound
Marrubium vulgare

2', introduced invasive, perennial

The species name says it all, this plant is vulgar. It moves into disturbed ground, spreads and displaces the natives that were there. Bees like it. It comes up very easily from seed. As for its alleged medicinal properties, I would just as soon buy cough drops. 9/4/15

170

Horsetail Milkweed
Asclepias subverticillata

3', native, perennial

Horsetail Milkweed has very narrow leaves.
It is good for carpenter bees and butterflies
— and extremely bad for livestock. 8/29/15

171

Horseweed
(Coulter's Horseweed)
Laennecia coulteri

3', native, annual

172

Horseweed leaves have teeth on the edges.
The flowers have no petals. This plant can
be toxic to cattle and goats. 8/25/15

Huachuca Mountain Rocktrumpet
(Sonoran Jasmine)
Mandevilla brachysiphon

173

18", native, perennial

Huachuca Mountain Rocktrumpet is not just another attractive plant with 1.5" trumpet-shaped white flowers, but it smells good, too. It really does have a jasmine fragrance. The seedpods look like long, skinny goat horns. This plant is often found on limey hillsides. 8/8/14

Jimsonweed
(Sacred Thornapple, Sacred Datura)
Datura wrightii

174

Jimsonweed grows to about 4' tall and as wide. Although the flowers are beautiful, you should avoid planting this plant if any children (or hippies) are around, as all parts are very poisonous. In the photo, you can see some insect damage caused by bugs that are immune to the poison. By ingesting Jimsonweed, they become unpalatable to many predators. 9/8/14

Long-Flowered Four O'Clock
(Sweet Four O'Clock)
Mirabilis longiflora

175

3'x3', native, perennial

Long-Flowered Four O'Clock flowers at night and is a favorite of the Sphinx Moth (Tomato Hornworm). The flowers are very fragrant. It is a tuberous plant. 7/15/14

Mala Mujer
(Bad Woman)
Cnidoscolus angustidens

3", native, perennial

Like a bad woman (or bad man), all parts of Mala Mujer should be left alone. The leaves and stems have stinging spines. The white milky sap is a powerful irritant. (Yes, I realize if a woman had named this plant, it would have probably been called Mala Muchacho). 4/1/05

Mariposa Lily
(Doubting Mariposa Lily)
Calochortus ambiguus

1', native, perennial

Mariposa Lily is a spring bloomer that grows from a bulb. It is very similar to another plant, Desert Mariposa, which is yellow or red. 4/13/14

177

Mexican Oregano
(Lemon Beebalm, Yerba de Montanas)

Monarda citriodora ssp. austromontana

178

2', native, annual/perennial

Mexican Oregano is one of the great plants of the grassland. It has tiers of whirled white flowers. The foliage is pungent and has been used in traditional cooking for ages. It tastes better than commercial oregano. Some enterprising person should put this plant in commercial production. 8/6/15

Mexican Star Lily
Milla biflora

18", native, perennial

If you see Mexican Star Lily blooming, it is a good thing because it indicates summer rains have started. No rain means no Mexican Stars. The flower is a pure, innocent white and smells a bit like lime when first open. Mexican Star grows from a corm. 8/22/14

179

Pepperweed
(Thurber's Pepperweed)
Lepidium thurberi

1', native, annual/perennial

180

Pepperweed can be found in disturbed areas.
In moist springs, it can cover large areas.
Botanically, Pepperweed is a mustard. 4/14/14

Prickly Poppy
(Southwestern Prickly Poppy,
Fried Egg Plant)

Argemone pleiacantha

3', native, perennial   **181**

Prickly Poppy is a striking plant whose flowers, from a distance, resemble a fried egg. It likes disturbed areas and roadsides, and can become a pest in some situations. Prickly Poppy grows from a fleshy root, which must be removed if you want to get rid of it. 5/18/14

Shrubby Buckwheat
(Bastardsage)
Eriogonum wrightii

2', native, perennial

182

Shrubby Buckwheat has grayish stems covered in hairs. Cattle and deer like to graze this plant. 8/13/15 *Rothrock Grama in background.*

Small Matweed
Guilleminea densa

2", native, perennial

Small Matweed is a low-growing, mat-forming plant with green, shiny leaves. The foliage turns reddish as it starts to dry out in the fall. 8/24/15

183

Snake Cotton
(Arizona Snake Cotton)
Froelichia arizonica

3', native, perennial

184

Snake Cotton is an upright-growing plant. The
flowers are cotton-like and held above the foliage.
The leaves are green on top and light-colored
underneath due to the presence of wooly hairs.
9/22/15

Sonoran Globe Amaranth
Gomphrena sonorae

2', native warm season annual

Sonoran Globe Amaranth can be a short-lived perennial on warm sites. 8/26/15

Spurge
Chamaesyce sp.

6", native, warm season annual

There are several spurges that grow in the grasslands. They are low growing, or prostrate, and have small white flowers and red stems. If you pinch a stem, sticky white sap will come out.
8/24/15

186

Tufted Evening Primrose

Oenothera caespitosa

8", native, perennial

187

Tufted Evening Primrose's flowers open in the early morning, fade to pink, and are done in the midday sun. A new crop replaces them the next day. It blooms in the spring and grows out from a fleshy root. 4/14/14

Tufted Globe Amaranth
Gomphrena caespitosa

6", native, perennial

188

Tufted Globe Amaranth is a plant that changes appearance. When it flowers in early spring, its leaves are a fuzzy gray-green. After flowering, the leaves turn a semi-gloss dark green. The plant then becomes a small rosette of dark green leaves. 4/12/15

White Girdlepod
Mitracarpus breviflorus

8", native, warm season annual

White Girdlepod is a small, easily overlooked forb that is part of the green carpet that comes up with summer rains. 8/29/15

189

White Milkwort
Polygala alba

18", native, perennial

White Milkwort flowers in the spring, where it really stands out from the grasses that haven't greened up yet. It can continue to flower with the summer rains. 6/9/15

190

White Prairie Clover
Dalea candida

3', native, perennial

White Prairie Clover is often found along roadsides or bank cuts. One reason it is successful in arid grasslands is that it packs a taproot longer than the aboveground growth. 8/6/15

191

Wild Balsam Apple
Echinopepon wrightii

6', warm season annual

192

Wild Balsam Apple is a climbing vine that likes sandy conditions. The diagnostic fruit is similar to Wild Cucumber, but Wild Balsam Apple's fruit is smaller and more elongated while the Cucumber's is rounded. 8/26/15

Annual Goldeneye

(Longleaf False Goldeneye)

Heliomeris longifolia

3', native, warm season annual

Annual Goldeneye can cover whole hillsides with its golden flowers in early fall. This plant can be toxic to livestock. 9/24/15

193

Annual Sunflower
(Common Sunflower)
Helianthus annuus

15', native, warm season annual

194

Annual Sunflower comes up with cool season rains but waits for summer moisture to do its big growth push. Doves and Finches eat the seeds in fall. 9/24/15

Annual Yellow Aster
(Slender Goldenweed)
Machaeranthera gracilis

1', native, warm season annual

Annual Yellow Aster grows close to the ground and gets covered in yellow blossoms. The stems on this plant are hairy. 8/13/15

195

Arizona Showflower
(Mexican Yellowshow)
Amoreuxia palmatifida

1', native, perennial

Arizona Showflower is one of the most striking plants in the grasslands. It blooms with the summer rains. Each blossom only last a short while. Arizona Showflower grows out of an underground tuber. 8/6/15

Bahia
(Hairyseed Bahia)
Bahia absinthifolia

1', native, perennial

Bahia is an attractive Forb that is often found in alkaline sites. The foliage is gray-green and trident-shaped at the tips. It is a good butterfly plant. 8/13/15 *(Tumbleweed in foreground)*

197

Buffalobur
(Buffalobur Nightshade)
Solanum rostratum

2', native, warm season annual

198

Buffalobur is an unpleasant plant covered with spines. The leaves are shaped like watermelon leaves and have spines down the veins. Not only are the spines sharp, they also contain an irritant. This plant is toxic to livestock and anything else that might consume it. 8/6/15

Buffalo Gourd
(Missouri Gourd, Stinking Gourd)
Cucurbita foetidissima

1' x 20', native, perennial

199

Buffalo Gourd has large spade-like leaves.
The fruits are green striped, drying to tan.
It grows from a large underground tuber that
stinks if you nick it in any way while digging.
Buffalo Gourd is similar to another gourd,
Finger Gourd, (not pictured) which has leaves that
look like fingers on a spread-out hand. 6/7/14

Camphorweed
Heterotheca subaxillaris

4', native, warm season annual

Camphorweed is often found by the roadside, or in disturbed areas. The leaves are sticky. Many consider it a weed. It is a good plant to attract butterflies and other insects. 9/24/15

200

Chocolate Flower
(Lyreleaf Greeneyes)
Berlandiera lyrata

1', native, perennial

201

Chocolate Flower is one of the gems of the grasslands. Sniff it early in the morning and you find it really does smell like chocolate. The leaves are said to resemble the old musical instrument the lyre. When the petals fall off, the center stays green. 4/14/14

Desert Marigold
Baileya multiradiata

2' x 2', native, cool season annual

Desert Marigold is a showy plant that can be perennial in warmer spots. It reseeds itself easily. The leaves almost appear silvery and are covered with small hairs. Desert Marigold is much hairier than Bahia. 8/26/15 *(Pigweed in background)*

202

Dwarf Prairie Clover
Dalea nana

1', native, perennial

Prairie Clovers are very hard to tell apart. They all have glands on the leaves. The yellow flowers of Dwarf Prairie Clover help ID it. 8/24/15

203

Echeandia
(Torrey's Craiglily)
Echeandia flavescens

1', native, perennial

Echeandia grows from fleshy roots (corms). The leaves appear grass-like. When the plant goes dormant in the fall, a cluster of thin brown leaves radiating out from a central area is left. 8/9/14

Fetid Marigold
Dyssodia papposa

1', native, warm season annual

Fetid Marigold is easiest identified by its pungent smell, especially if you brush up against it. Some like it, some don't. It turns a coppery color as it cures in the fall. 9/24/15

Goathead
(Puncturevine)
Tribulus terrestris

2" tall x 2' wide, introduced, warm season annual

206

Goathead is the plant we all love to hate. It has very stiff spines on its seedhead that penetrate tires and thin-soled footwear. An extract of Goathead is used as a male enhancement product. Go figure. 9/4/15

Golden Crownbeard
Verbesina encelioides

3', native, warm season annual

Golden Crownbeard likes disturbed areas. It can flower from early spring to late fall, depending on moisture. This plant contains alkaloids and can be toxic to grazing livestock. In warm conditions it can survive more than a year. 8/24/15

Goldenrod
(Missouri Goldenrod)
Solidago missouriensis

3', native, perennial

Goldenrod is a summer and fall bloomer that likes some shade. It often grows in clusters and attracts butterflies. 10/5/15

Green's Lotus
(Greene's Bird-foot Trefoil)
Lotus greenei

6" x 2', native, perennial

Green's Lotus is a spring bloomer – if there has been sufficient winter moisture. The flowers are yellow with coral backs. As the flowers mature, more coral shows. This plant makes a good groundcover. 4/12/15

Hopi Tea
(Hopi Tea Greenthread)
Thelesperma megapotamicum

2', Native, Perennial

Hopi Tea is a very wiry plant that at first glance
appears leafless. The flowers have no petals.
It has been cultivated for use as a drink. 4/14/14

Hymenothrix
(Trans-Pecos Thimblehead)
Hymenothrix wislizeni

3', native, warm season annual

Hymenothrix is a spindly plant that can live up to two years. It is common and can flower from early summer through fall. 8/6/15

Longstalk Chinchweed
Pectis longipes

6", native, perennial

Longstalk Chinchweed is a small sun-loving plant with a long blooming season. The flowers have a spicy fragrance. 4/12/15

212

Mariposa Lily
(Desert Mariposa Lily)
Calochortus kennedyi

1', native, perennial

Mariposa Lily grow from a bulb and
bloom in spring, provided there was enough
winter moisture. This plant can also be orange.
The word mariposa means butterfly. 4/13/14

213

Melon Loco
Apondanthera undulata

1' tall but up to 10' wide, native, perennial

Melon Loco is a sprawling gourd. It is distinctive because its fruit is ribbed. 8/13/15

Mountain Gromwell
(Smooththroat Stoneseed)
Lithospermum cobrense

1', native, perennial

215

Mountain Gromwell is found in the higher locations of the grasslands. It has slender, hairy leaves and is usually an understory plant under oaks. 8/6/15

Mountain Oxeye
Heliopsis parvifolia

2' x 2', native, perennial

Mountain Oxeye has yellow daisy-like flowers about 2" across. Good butterfly attractor. 8/6/15 *(Johnsongrass growing up through plant)*

216

Mullein
(Common Mullein)
Verbascum thapsus

6', introduced, biennial

Mullein is found in disturbed soils. It takes two years to bloom, then dies. The first year, it forms a rosette of leaves. The leaves are very hairy and resistant to most grazing animals. 8/6/15

217

New Mexico Birds-foot Trefoil
Lotus plebeius

218

1', Native, Perennial

New Mexico Birds-foot Trefoil has narrowly lobed gray-green leaves with three fingers. Like Greene's Lotus, it has yellow and coral flowers. It is a more upright plant than Greene's Lotus and blooms from spring to fall. 8/6/15

Pectis
(Spreading Chichweed)
Pectis prostrata

6", native, warm season annual

A small plant, which could easily be overlooked, unless you were looking closely at the grassland ground. In a good year it helps turn hillsides green. 8/29/15

219

Plains Flax
Linum puberulum

1', native, warm season annual

Plains Flax has thin, wiry-looking stems that are covered in small hairs. The petals in some individual plants make a more completed bowl shape than the ones we have in the photos. 8/6/15

220

Rocky Mountain Zinnia
Zinnia grandiflora

8" x 2', native, perennial

Rocky Mountain Zinnia is composed of many
small branches. It has a long flowering period.
The center of the flower is orangish. It can spread
by rhizomes. This is a good landscape plant. 8/6/15

221

Rosary Bean
(Texas Snoutbean)
Rhynchosia senna

1' x 3', native, perennial

222

Rosary Bean is a vining forb with yellow
pea-shaped flowers. The veins are visible
on the leaves. 10/5/15

Rothrock's Crownbeard
Verbesina rothrockii

2', native, perennial

223

Rothhrock's Crownbeard is only found in the US in a handful of southern counties in Arizona and New Mexico. The leaves feel like 100 grit sandpaper. It likes limey sites. Notice the gray limestone rocks in the picture. 9/4/15

Rough Blackfoot
Melampodium sericeum

2', native, warm season annual

Rough Blackfoot is one of the most common summer annuals while being one of the most unnoticed. It is upright growing and its yellow flower is about a quarter-inch wide. 9/24/15

San Pedro Daisy
Lasianthaea podocephala

1', native, perennial

San Pedro Daisy has rough feeling leaves and
usually is found on hillsides. The plant grows from
a series of fleshy roots, which might remind you
of a plant tarantula if you dug them up. 8/6/15

225

San Pedro Matchweed
Xanthocephalum gymnospermoides

4', native, warm season annual

226

San Pedro Matchweed is seldom seen alone. It usually is found in large colonies at the bottom of hills or in draws, where it makes large bands of color. It blooms earlier and is more orange than Annual Goldeneye, which also makes large color patches. This plant is very good for attracting butterflies. 8/24/15

Sanvitalia
(Abert's Creeping Zinnia)
Sanvitalia abertii

1', native, warm season annual

Sanvitalia flower only has petals (rays) on the outside of the floral disc. The leaves show 3 veins. It flowers in summer or early fall. 8/13/15

Sensitive Partridge Pea
Chamaecrista nictitans

1', native, annual

Sensitive Partridge Pea is a common grasslands plant with small fernlike foliage. In warm conditions it can overwinter. When dried out, it turns reddish-brown. 8/26/15

228

Showy Goldeneye
Heliomeris multiflora

4', native, perennial

Showy Goldeneye is often found growing on rocky outcrops, especially limestone. The flowers are similar to Toothed Goldeneye but are narrower and glossier. The genus *Heliomeris* means "part of the sun." 10/3/15

229

Sida
(Spreading Fanpetals)
Sida abutifolia

6" x 18", native, perennial

230

Sida is a small trailing plant that flowers from spring to fall. The flowers are 1" across and open up best in the afternoon. Sida is the plant that is found on more soil types and locations than any other in the grasslands. 10/14/15

Slender Blanketfower
(Slender Blanketflower)
Gaillardia pinnatifida

1', native, perennial

The leaves of this plant are covered with hairs.
It is another good butterfly attractant. 4/12/15

231

Stickleaf

(Isolated Blazingstar)

Mentzelia sp.

2', native, warm season annual

232

Stickleaf (two species pictured) really lives up to its name. Seedpods also stick. Stickleaf prefers to grow in sandy sites. 8/26/15

Sundrops
(Hartwegg's Sundrops)
Calylophus hartwegii

1' x 2', native, perennial

Sundrops is a very good landscape plant that attracts butterflies and other pollinators. The flowers turn orange after about a day. Long blooming season. 6/9/15

233

Tomatillo
(Ivyleaf Groundcherry)
Physalis hederifolia

2', native, perennial

234

Tomatillo produces a lantern like fruit that turns tan when dried. The flowers are a drab yellow. 9/30/15

Toothleaf Goldeneye
Viguiera dentata

6', native, perennial

Toothleaf Goldeneye flowers in the fall with typical Goldeneye flowers. It differs from other Goldeneyes by having much larger triangular-shaped leaves with teeth on the edges. It is usually found growing under larger plants. 9/24/15

235

Twinleaf Senna
Senna bauhinioides

18", native, perennial

Twinleaf Senna has hairy leaves that are paired. The flowers, which can bloom from spring to late summer, attract butterflies. 10/5/15

236

Arizona Poppy
(Caltrop)
Kallstroemia grandiflora

1' x 3', native, warm season annual

Arizona Poppy has flowers that are almost two-and-a-half inches across. It blooms with summer moisture and attracts butterflies. It is also larval food for caterpillars. It is easy to propagate Arizona Poppy from seed. 8/29/15

237

Smallflowered Arizona Poppy
(Warty Caltrop)
Kallstroemia parviflora

1' x2', native, warm season annual

Smallflowered Arizona Poppy is a ground-hugging small vine. The yellow–orange flowers are less than an inch in diameter. It is often confused with Goathead, which has more of a pure yellow flower and a smaller and tighter leaf structure. 9/4/15

238

Arizona Sunflowerweed
Tithonia thurberi

5', native, warm season annual

Arizona Sunflowerweed has smaller flowers than the more commonly sold *Tithonia*, Mexican Sunflower. It is found growing under other larger plants and would make a good cultivar. 8/26/15 *(Gulf Fritillary Butterfly)*

239

Butterflyweed
(Butterfly Milkweed)
Asclepias tuberosa

3', native, perennial

In addition to being a very beautiful plant, Buterflyweed is a very important food plant for Monarch and other butterflies. As its botanical name implies, it grows from an underground tuber. If you can, plant some of these plants or sow some seed. This is a great "use it twice" plant. 8/29/15 *(Common Buckeye Butterfly)*

Foothill Deervetch
Lotus humistratus

2" x 6", native, cool season annual

Foothill Deervetch is a hairy, mat-forming plant. Its flowers are yellow, turning to orange. High foliage to flower ratio. 4/12/15

241

Hummingbird Trumpet
Epilobium canum ssp. latifolium

2' x 3', native, perennial

242

Hummingbird Trumpet grows in canyon washes. It blooms from summer until the first hard frost. Excellent hummingbird and butterfly plant. The branches are brittle and break off easily.10/3/15

Indian Paintbrush
Castilleja sp.

1', native

There are several species of Indian Paintbrush in the grasslands. They have an upright growth habit. Paintbrushes are parasitic while still carrying on some of their own photosynthesis. It is kind of like having a bad relative living in your house that dusts off the TV once in a while. 8/6/15

243

Low Rattlebox
Crotalaria pumila

2', native, warm season annual

Low Rattlebox can be a perennial in warmer sites. When brushed up against, the dried grape-shaped seedpods make a noise like a rattlesnake. While a lot of folks have jumped when mistaking Low Rattlebox for a snake, I don't believe anyone has ever mistaken a rattlesnake for Low Rattlebox. 8/26/15

Poreleaf Dogweed
Adenophyllum porophyllum

2', native, perennial

Poreleaf Dogweed is a very upright growing plant whose population numbers seem to be on the increase in recent years. It has an unfortunate name and underachieving flowers that look like they should open up but never do. 9/24/15

Red Zinnia
(Peruvian Zinnia)
Zinnia peruviana

2', native, warm season annual

246

Red Zinnia is an upright, pretty plant that likes some shade. It is only found in three counties in Arizona. It reliably comes back from seed and attracts pollinators, especially butterflies. 8/29/15

Scarlet Bugler
(Beardlip Penstemon)
Penstemon barbatus

3', native, perennial

Scarlet Bugler blooms in the spring during the hummingbird migration and again in the summer. It is usually found on north-facing slopes or in partial shade. 7/30/15

247

Scarlet Creeper
(Trans- Pecos Morning-glory)
Ipomea cristulata

6', native, warm season annual

248

Scarlet Creeper is a common summer annual that climbs up fences or other vegetation. Hummingbirds seek it out. It differs from most other Morning Glories because its flowers stay open all day. 8/29/15

Scarlet Globemallow
Sphaeralcea coccinea

3', native, perennial

Scarlet Globemallow has gray-green deeply divided leaves and orange flowers that attract pollinators. It can spread by rhizomes. 4/13/14

249

Scarlet Spiderling
Boerhavia coccinea

4', native, perennial

Scarlet Spiderling is a spreading plant that will lean on other plants or structure if given a chance. As with other Spiderlings, its stems are sticky. 8/13/15

Screw U
(Wislizenus's False Threadleaf)
Schkuhria pinnata
var. guatemalensis

2', native, warm season annual

Okay, I admit it. This one has been included because I like the common name, which is a shortened version of its almost unpronounceable genus. 9/24/15

Shrubby Copperleaf
Acalypha phleoides

2', native, perennial

Shrubby Copperleaf is a low-growing plant that can get 2' wide. It is notable for its red flowering structures. There are several species of annual Copperleafs whose foliage turns reddish late in summer. 8/29/15

252

Shrubby Purslane
Portulaca suffrutescens

1', native, perennial

Shrubby Purslane has succulent leaves and comes back every year from tuberous roots. 8/26/15

253

Snapdragon Vine
(Roving Sailor*)
Maurandella antirrhiniflora

8', Native, Perennial

254

Snapdragon Vine can have either purple or red flowers. It grows in northern or shaded exposures and attracts hummingbirds. 10/5/15

*This is possibly one of the worst common names I have ever heard.

Supine Bean
Macroptilium supinum

6" x 3', native, perennial

What is interesting about this plant is that in addition to the orange flowers that are held above the stems, Supine Bean also produces underground flowers that never see the light of day. Most seed production comes from the unpollinated underground flowers. Plants with this type of seed production are called obligate selfers. This plant grows as an understory. 8/8/14

Texas Betony
(Scarlet Hedgenettle)
Stachys coccinea

3', native, perennial

256

Texas Betony likes moist canyon bottoms.
It flowers from spring to fall with bright
red flowers that attract hummingbirds. 10/5/15

Arizona Blue Eyes
(Wild Dwarf Morning-glory)
Evolvulus arizonicus

1', native, perennial

Arizona Blue Eyes is a common grasslands wildflower. The flower is about three-quarters of an inch wide. It blooms from spring through fall. Silver Dwarf Morning-glory is a similar looking plant but has gray leaves and a white flower. 8/8/14

257

Arizona Bluecurls
Trichostema arizonicum

2', native, perennial

Arizona Bluecurls has a beautiful small flower, about an inch across. It blooms from early summer through fall. If this flower were larger it would put petunias out of business. 8/16/14

258

Bluedicks
Dichelostemma capitatum

1', native, perennial

Bluedicks can send up leaves in late fall and flowers in early spring. Each individual flower is about an inch wide. They grow from an edible bulb. 3/27/14

259

Cochise Beardtongue
Penstemon dasyphyllus

18", native, perennial

Cochise Beartdtoungue is found only in the border counties of southeastern Arizona, one county in southwestern New Mexico, and a couple of counties in southwestern Texas. It blooms in the spring and likes caliche soils. If you are looking at a penstemon and those conditions are not met, you are probably looking at a different penstemon. 4/14/14

260

Dakota Verbena
(Dakota Mock Vervain)
Glandularia bipinnatifida

18" x 2', native, perennial

Dakota Verbena has one of the longest blooming seasons in the grasslands. I have seen it bloom in February and continue all the way to December. Like most verbenas, it attracts butterflies. 4/12/15

261

Dayflower
(Whitemouth Dayflower)
Commelina erecta

18", native, perennial

262

Dayflower has a showy flower with three petals. The lower petal is whitish and smaller than the other two. It flowers with the summer rains until fall. This plant is similar to Birdbill Dayflower, which has three blue petals of equal size. 9/4/15

Dyschoriste
(Spreading Snakeherb)
Dyschoriste schiedeana var. decumbens

6" x 1', native, perennial

Dyschoriste is a long blooming, April to October, low-growing plant with attractive purple flowers. The flowers are about an inch across. With a little supplemental irrigation I believe the flower to foliage ratio would improve. It would make for a nice native groundcover in a landscape. 8/16/14

Gilia
(Macomb's Ipomopsis)
Ipomopsis macombii

2', native, perennial

There are several types of Gilias in the grasslands that all have long, tube-shaped, purple flowers and bloom from summer to fall. They are good hummingbird plants. 8/29/15

Gregg's Mistflower
(Palmleaf Thoroughwort)
Conoclinium gregii

2', native, perennial

Gregg's Mistflower is another great plant if you are interested in attracting Monarch butterflies. If you think it looks like a Eupatorium, you are right. It was one until the name change. 9/4/15

Ivyleaf Morning-glory
Ipomoea hederacea

8', introduced, annual

Ivyleaf Morning-glory is a climbing vine. It appears everywhere after the summer rains start. The flowers range from blue to purple and are about two inches across. 9/7/13

266

Locoweed
(Sheep Milkvetch)
Astragalus nothoxys

6" x 2', native, annual/perennial

Locoweed flowers in the spring and in a strong year can turn whole hillsides or bottoms purple. It can be very toxic to cattle and horses, causing a selenium poisoning. If enough other feed is available they will usually avoid it. 4/12/15

Mesa Tansyaster
Machaeranthera tagetina

18", native, warm season annual

Mesa Tansyaster starts to grow with the summer rains. It can continue its bloom into fall. It has a sparse ring of outer purple petals. The yellow floral center protrudes. 8/13/15

Mexican Passionflower
Passiflora mexicana

20', native, perennial

Mexican Passionflower climbs up other vegetation or rock faces. The flowers come in either purple or red. Although not as spectacular as some of the cultivated Passionflowers, they give off a light sweet smell when in bloom. This is an important host plant for the Western Gulf Fritillary Butterfly. 8/26/15

269

New Mexico Vervain
(Hillside Vervain)
Verbena neomexicana

3', native, perennial

New Mexico Vervain is a very upright-growing plant most often found growing on limey hillsides. 9/4/15 *(Ragweed in the background)*

Pinewoods Spiderwort
Tradescantia pinetorum

16", native, perennial

Pinewoods Spiderwort has slender grass-like leaves and blooms with the summer rains. The flower looks similar to Dayflowers, which have wider leaves. 8/9/14

Purple Prairie Clover
Dalea sp.

18", native, perennial

The herbaceous daleas are common plants and really hard to tell apart. The one pictured is Bearded Prairie Clover (Dalea pogonathera). They all put some nitrogen in the soil and attract insect pollinators. 8/24/15

272

San Pedro Ticktrefoil
Desmodium batocaulon

5', native, perennial

San Pedro Ticktrefoil is a vine that has deep green leaves with light central veins. The purple flowers are held above the foliage. This would make a nice bedding plant. The seeds are covered with barbed hairs and stick to pant legs, pets, or most anything that comes in contact with them. It likes some shade. 8/29/15

273

Sawtooth Sage
Salvia subincisa

10", native, warm season annual

Sawtooth Sage blooms with an attractive blue
flower that occurs after the summer rains start.
They look good when growing in a cluster.
The leaves are toothed. 9/4/15

274

Silverleaf Nightshade
Solanum elaeagnifolium

2', native, perennial

Silverleaf Nightshade is another of the life lesson plants. Some folks want to take it in and cultivate it because of its pretty purple flowers. That would be a mistake. The leaves and seedpods are poisonous. And when you try to pull it to get rid of it, you will find that the stems are spiny and the plant spreads underground runners. Don't encourage it. 8/24/15

Sonoran Beardtongue
Penstemon stenophyllus

2', Native, Perennial

Sonoran Beardtongue is a large flowered
Penstemon that is often found under oaks.
It flowers in late summer. It has a similar range
as Cochise Beardtongue but flowers later and is
not found on strictly caliche conditions. It is a good
plant for attracting bees and bumblebees. 8/29/15

Tanseyleaf Tansyaster
Machaeranthera tanacetifolia

3', native, warm season annual

Tanseyleaf Tansyaster is similar to
Mesa Tansyaster but is has the potential
to be a larger plant with bigger flowers. It
also has a more upright growth habit. 8/13/15

277

Thistle
Cirsium sp.

4', native, biennial/perennial

There are several thistles that make their home in the grasslands. They all have spines on their leaves. Some may become invasive. All of them do a great job of attracting multiple species of butterflies. 8/29/15 *(Pipevine Swallowtail Butterfly)*

Trailing Four O'Clock
(Trailing Windmills)
Allionia incarnata

5', native, annual/perennial

Trailing Four O'Clock can be perennial in warm conditions. It has sticky hairy leaves and stems. The bloom season can last from spring to fall. 8/13/15

279

Tripleleaf Morning-glory
Ipomea ternifolia

3', native, warm season annual

Tripleleaf Morning-glory has large (over two inches) flowers that come in pink, lavender, and white shades. 8/26/15

280

Velvetseed Milkwort
Polygala obscura

1', native, perennial

Velvetseed Milkwort is another of the plants you will really appreciate… if you get down on ground level and check it out closely. The seedheads are disc-shaped. 8/6/15

281

Woodsorrel
(Drummond's Woodsorrel)
Oxalis drummondii

5", *native, perennial*

Woodsorrel grows from a bulb that is sought-after by Mearn's quail as a food source. There are a couple of pink-blooming Woodsorrels in the grasslands. This one blooms in the fall. 8/29/15

282

Wooly Loco
(Wooly Locoweed)
Astragalus mollissimus

10", native, perennial

Wooly Loco has gray-green leaves and blooms in the spring with violet colored flower. The leaves are covered in small hairs, giving it a soft appearance. Wooly Loco is poisonous to most grazing livestock. 2/26/15

283

Abert's Buckwheat
Eriogonum abertianum

1', native, cool season annual

Abert's Buckwheat has flowers that start white but turn pink as they mature. It likes sandy or silty soils. 4/20/14

284

Annual Buckwheat
(Sorrel Buckwheat)
Eriogonum polycladon

1' – 2', native, warm season annual

Annual Buckwheat usually grows in clusters in or along dry washes. It gets used in dry flower arrangements. 8/13/15

285

Brownfoot Acourtia
Acourtia wrightii

3', native, perennial

Brownfoot blooms late into fall with a honey scented flower. It is a good butterfly plant that likes rocky hillsides. 10/3/15

286

Crested Anoda
Anoda cristata

2', native, warm season annual

Crested Anoda has a splash of red along the main vein of its leaves. The seed capsule is very distinctive. 8/29/15

Desert Holly
(Dwarf Desertpeony)
Acourtia nana

6", native, perennial

Desert Holly flowers with a fragrant pink bloom in the spring. The leaves are unique. It is usually found at the base of mesquites or other shrubs. 8/13/5

Devil's Claw
(Doubleclaw)
Proboscidea parviflora

3' x 4', native, warm season annual

289

Devil's Claw is recognizable by its fruit that, when ripe, splits open and hooks on the fur or legs of passersby. This means of seed dispersal started back in the days of megafauna (mammoths, mastodons, etc.) The ripe fruit is gray. Devil's Claw seeds are edible. Leaves and stems are sticky. 8/6/15

Horsetail Vine
(Texas Bindweed)
Convolvulus equitans

3', native, warm season annual

The gray-green leaves of Horsetail Vine are shaped like spearheads. In warmer locations it can be a perennial. 8/6/15

Huachuca Mountain Morning-glory
Ipomea plummerae

1', native, perennial

Huachuca Mountain Morning-glory has flowers that open to about one inch. They are usually a deep pink color, but occasionally you will see a white one. This plant grows from a tuber about the size of a Hershey's Kiss. 8/19/14

Jatropha
(Ragged Nettlespurge)
Jatropha macrorhiza

2', native, perennial

Jatropha emerges in the springtime with a set of pink flowers. Maple (or some would say marijuana) -looking leaves soon follow. Jatropha grows from a large tuber. All parts of this plant are poisonous. 5/21/14

Parry Penstemon
(Parry's Beardtongue)
Penstemon parryi

3', native, perennial

Parry Penstemon is a spring blooming penstemon that attracts hummingbirds. It is common in the elevations of the lower deserts. 3/6/15

293

Ribbon Four O'Clock
(Narrowleaf Four O'Clock)
Mirabilis linearis

3', native, perennial

Ribbon Four O'Clock has striking neon pink flowers that often appear in spring when everything else is still dormant. It can flower through the early fall. Ribbon Four O'clock grows from a tuber. 4/28/14

Rougeplant
Rivina humilis

3', native, perennial

Rougeplant is best known for its bright red
berries, which follow stalks of light pink flowers.
The berries are eaten by birds but don't try them,
as they are poisonous to people. Rougeplant
is an understory plant. 8/26/15

Southwestern Cosmos
Cosmos parviflorus

30", native, warm season annual

Southwestern Cosmos have a light pink or white flower that is about an inch wide. The flower is followed by some nasty seeds that are among the worst offenders in the 'sock-sticker' category. 8/29/15 *(Morning-glory and Alligator Juniper berries)*

Tufted Milkweed
Asclepias nummularia

8", native, perennial

Tufted Milkweed has blue-green foliage that looks almost succulent. Like most milkweeds, it is beneficial to Monarch butterflies. 5/10/14

297

Velvetweed
Oenothera curtiflora

6', native, perennial

Velvetweed is often found on the roadside, in moist pockets, or other places that receive extra water. When in bloom, the flowering structure resembles a lizard's tail. 9/4/15

298

Glossary

alkaline soil – Soil that has high pH and low fertility. These soils usually have poor drainage and are light in color.

caliche – A layer of soil that has been cemented together by calcium carbonate. It is usually light colored, allows little water percolation, and is very alkaline.

corm – An underground storage stem similar to a bulb. To tell a corm from a bulb, cut it in half. The bulb will have layers and a corm will be solid.

limey soils – Soil formed from the breakdown of limestone rock. It has high pH. All limey soils are alkaline, but all alkaline soils are not limey.

nodes – The joints of a plant stem or stalk.

pollinator plant – Any plant that attracts bees, bumblebees, butterflies or hummingbirds.

rhizomes – Underground roots that surface and make new plants. No need to mess around with pollination and seed. See Bermuda and Ragweed.

sp. – Species. Often used as a "get out of jail" card when the exact species isn't known. Also used when several species look and act very similar, and splitting them out isn't practical for most folks.

tuber – Underground fleshy stems that hold moisture and nutrients. Tubers are an excellent strategy for survival in areas with long periods of drought, as a plant can take in moisture and nutrients when abundant and save it for an extended period. They lack the basal plates that the roots grow from, which bulbs and corms have.

understory – A growing area that is sheltered and protected by larger vegetation.

References

Allred, Kelly. *A Field Guide to the Grasses of New Mexico.* Las Cruces, NM: Department of Agricultural Communications, 2005.

Coronado RC & D Area Inc. and Conservation Districts of Southeastern Arizona. *Grasses of Southeastern Arizona.* 2006.

---. *Poisonous Plants of Southeastern Arizona.* 2006.

---. *Shrubs of Southeastern Arizona.* 2006.

---. *Summer Forbs of Southeastern Arizona.* 2006.

---. *Trees of Southeastern Arizona.* 2006.

---. *Winter Forbs of Southeastern Arizona.* 2006.

Dimmitt, Mark and Ken Asplund. "The Desert Grasslands." *Sonorensis,* summer (1990) : 14–15.

Earle, W. Hubert. *Cacti of the Southwest.* Tempe, AZ: Rancho Arroyo Book Distributor, 1990.

Epple, Anne, Lewis Epple and John Wiens. *A Field Guide to the Plants of Arizona.* 2nd ed. Helena, MT: Falcon Publishing, 2012.

Humphrey, Robert. *Arizona Range Grasses,* Edited by George Ruyle and Deborah Young. Tucson: University of Arizona Press, 2003.

Kearney, Thomas H. and Robert Peebles. *Arizona Flora.* Berkeley: University of California Press, 1960.

Kinsey, T. Beth, "Southeastern Arizona Wildflowers and Plants." *Firefly Forest.* Last modified 2016. http://www.fireflyforest.com/flowers

Kleinman, Russ. "Vascular Plants of the Gila Wilderness." *Western New Mexico University Department of Natural Sciences & The Dale A. Zimmerman Herbarium.* Last modified 2015. http://wnmu.edu/academic/nspages/gilaflora

McClaran, Mitchel P. and Thomas R. Van Devender. *The Desert Grassland.* Tucson: University of Arizona Press, 1995.

Milinovitch, Maggie Moe. *Wildflowers: A Field Guide to the Flowering Plants of Southern Arizona.* Arivaca, AZ: Connection, 2011.

"Plants Database." *United States Department of Agriculture National Resource Conservation Service.* Last modified January 25, 2016. http://plants.usda.gov

"SEINet Arizona Chapter." National Science Foundation. Accessed [12/1/15 – 12/18/15]. http://www.swbiodiversity.org/seinet

Sturla, Gene, "Southwest Desert Flora," Last modified 2015. http://southwestdesertflora.com

Van Devender, Thomas. "History of the Dessert Grassland." *Sonorensis,* summer (1990): 16–19.

Acknowledgements

You wouldn't be holding this book in your hands if it wasn't for the combined efforts of a lot of folks. I should start by saying Dale was more important to this project than me. We sure had a lot of fun cruising around, telling stories and taking some pictures. Well over 3500 photos were taken for this book. I think we told 3600 stories. Some were even true. It is my sincere hope that anyone who partners up on a project has as much fun and as enjoyable an experience as I did working with Dale.

Linda Kennedy's and Dan Robinett's knowledge about all things grassland is exceeded only by their patience and willingness to share that knowledge. Much of what is written in this book is channeled directly from them. They deserve some credit for authorship but not the blame for bad jokes.

In addition to Linda's and Dan's help with plant identification I also got help from Peter Gierlach, Iris Rodden, Kim McReynolds, George Montgomery, and many others. The final decision of what to call a plant was mine so don't blame them if you disagree with something. The butterflies were identified by Robert Behrstock. Much of my seed information through the years has come from Gary Mascarnic. He was doing native seed long before native seed was cool.

Rancher Walt Meyers was the first to take me out and start to train me in Rangeland Monitoring. His lovely and talented daughter Katie Cline has done a lot to continue that training through the years. Walt and George Ruyle also stood up for me when it came to deciding if my monitoring work could be accepted by other agencies. I sure appreciated that.

It is really popular to bash all things government these days but here is something you should be aware of. Some of the most dedicated, conservation orientated folks I have been associated with work for local government agencies. There has been nothing but good experiences working with the local Forest Service, University of Arizona Cooperative Extension Service, and National Resource Conservation Service (NRCS). I especially like the NRCS message of "Conservation through Cooperation". It is unfortunate that these local folks are hamstrung by the trickle down bureaucracy.

Faith Burkins-Gimzek had the unenviable task of trying to translate what I had written into some readable form of the English language. Jon Kandel put the whole project together. He did great work keeping the quality level where we hoped to be. Many thanks to Faith and Jon. This book literally would not have happened with them.

All the hand modeling was done by the author. If you are interested in hiring him to model your products please have your people call our people and we will see if we can work something out.

Biographies

Dale Armstrong *Photographer*

Dale is a retired hydrogeologist from Sonoita, Arizona with a professional career spanning over four decades and several countries. He is now a semi-professional photographer providing photographic services to the general public. His interest in photography began at an early age, starting with Kodak and AGFA 35mm film cameras. He now uses Nikon cameras and lenses. The DSLR cameras used for the photos in this book were the D7000, D7100, and 810. The lenses used for these photos were all Nikon consisting of : AF-S 24-70mm f/2.8 G ED, AF-S 70-200mm f/2.8 GII ED VR, AF-S 10-24mm f/2.8 G ED VR. All photographs were captured in RAW (NEF) format and processed in Adobe® Lightroom® 6.x.

Dale tells how this project came about came about:

> Dale and Jim's friendship started back in 2001 when early discussions about drought-tolerant Fremont Cottonwood trees and their effects on climate change during the last Ice Age lead to a simple wager. Having lost the bet with Jim, Dale was contractually obligated to follow Jim on many life-threatening excursions into the grassland wilderness of southeastern Arizona in attempts to capture the elusive Eragrostis lehmanniana and other such novel grasses, forbs, trees and succulents, some of which are not invasive. Three years of treacherous fieldtrips were required to finalize this life's work into an easy-to-understand book filled with elusive but valuable information for anyone willing to read the book.

Jim Koweek *Author*

Jim graduated from the University of Arizona in 1978 with a degree in Speech Communication. Upon signing on with a local landscape company, this degree proved a tremendous help with his first task – digging ditches for salvaged cactus. Since then, he has worked with native plants, seed and rock in Southern Arizona. All his botanical knowledge is field acquired. At one time he was a columnist and owned a plant nursery.

Currently, Jim lives in a canyon in mountains near the Mexican border that receives more than one hundred frosts a year. He is the owner and sole employee of Arizona Revegetation & Monitoring Co., which specializes in native grass restoration projects and native seed sales. Jim can often be found at local watering holes playing the mandolin.

Other publications include *Just Add Water – The Realistic Guide to the Land, Landscaping, and Gardening in The Higher Elevations of the Great Southwest.*

Jim can be contacted at jim@azreveg.com.

Index of Common Names

Index of
Official Common Names